AN ANECDOTAL HISTORY
OF INTERVARSITY PRESS, 1947-2007

HEART.

SOUL.

MIND.

STRENGTH.

Andrew T. Le Peau
and Linda Doll

FOREWORD BY Robert Fryling

IVP Books

An imprint of InterVarsity Press
Downers Grove, Illinois

InterVarsity Press
P.O. Box 1400, Downers Grove, IL 60515-1426
World Wide Web: www.ivpress.com
E-mail: mail@ivpress.com

InterVarsity Press® is the book-publishing division of InterVarsity Christian Fellowship/USA®, a student movement active on campus at hundreds of universities, colleges and schools of nursing in the United States of America, and a member movement of the International Fellowship of Evangelical Students. For information about local and regional activities, write Public Relations Dept., InterVarsity Christian Fellowship/USA, 6400 Schroeder Rd., P.O. Box 7895, Madison, WI 53707-7895, or visit the IVCF website at <www.intervarsity.org>.

All Scripture quotations, unless otherwise indicated, are taken from the New Revised Standard Version of the Bible, copyright 1989 by the Division of Christian Education of the National Council of the Churches in the USA. Used by permission. All rights reserved.

Design: Cindy Kiple
Cover image: istockphoto.com

ISBN-10: 0-8308-3369-2
ISBN-13: 978-0-8308-3369-6

Printed in the United States of America ∞

Library of Congress Cataloging-in-Publication Data

LePeau, Andrew T., 1952-
  Heart, soul, mind, strength: an anecdotal history of InterVarsity
Press, 1947-2007 / Andrew T. LePeau and Linda Doll.
    p. cm.
Includes bibliographical references and index.
ISBN-13: 978-0-8308-3369-6 (pbk.: alk. paper)
ISBN-10: 0-8308-3369-2 (pbk.: alk. paper)
  1. InterVarsity Press—History. 2. Publishers and
publishing—Illinois—Westmont—History. 3. Christian
literature—Publishing—United States—History. 4.
Evangelicalism—United States—History—20th century. I. Doll,
Linda, 1935- II. Title.
Z473.I68L42 2006
070.509773'24—dc22

                                                                      2006030483

P	20	19	18	17	16	15	14	13	12	11	10	9	8	7	6	5	4	3	2	1
Y	22	21	20	19	18	17	16	15	14	13	12	11	10	09	08	07	06			

To Jim Nyquist and Jim Sire,

friends and mentors

"When you sell a man a book

you don't sell him just twelve ounces of paper and ink and glue—

you sell him a whole new life."

CHRISTOPHER MORLEY

(QUOTED IN AN EARLY 1970S IVP CATALOG)

"We must absorb history . . . to know who we are and how we should act."

LESZEK KOLAKOWSKI

Table of Contents

Abbreviations

AAR	American Academy of Religion
ACCS	Ancient Christian Commentary on Scripture
ACDS	Ancient Christian Doctrine Series
ACTS	Ancient Christian Texts Series
BOD	Book of the Day
CAPS	Christian Association for Psychological Studies
CBA	Christian Booksellers Association
CICCU	Cambridge Inter-Collegiate Christian Union
CIS	Computing Information Services
CT	*Christianity Today*
DC	distribution center
ECPA	Evangelical Christian Publishers Association
ECPO	Evangelical Christian Publishing Overseas
ETS	Evangelical Theological Society
HSP	Harold Shaw Publishers
IBR	Institute for Biblical Research
ID	intelligent design
ICRS	International Christian Retail Show
IFES	International Fellowship of Evangelical Students
IV	InterVarsity
IVCF	InterVarsity Christian Fellowship
IVF	Inter-Varsity Fellowship
IVP	InterVarsity Press

IVP-UK	Inter-Varsity Press of the United Kingdom
IVP-US	InterVarsity Press of the United States
IVR	InterVarsity Records
JCN	*Journal of Christian Nursing*
NBC	*New Bible Commentary*
NBD	*New Bible Dictionary*
NCF	Nurses Christian Fellowship
OICCU	Oxford Inter-Collegiate Christian Union
PBT	Permanent Book Table
RCS	Reformation Commentary on Scripture
SAC	Staff Advisory Council of IVCF
SBL	Society of Biblical Literature
SLJ	*Student Leadership Journal*

Sidebars

Foreword

I am honored to write a foreword to this informative and inspiring story of InterVarsity Press—for it is a story that has profoundly affected my life.

InterVarsity Press (IVP) and I were both born in 1947, but my first conscious awareness of InterVarsity Press came many years later when I was in high school. At that time my older brother, John, was involved with Inter-Varsity Christian Fellowship (IVCF) as a student at the University of Pennsylvania and started bringing home HIS magazine and IVP books for me to read. One was the booklet *Quiet Time,* which initiated a daily devotional practice for me that has continued ever since.

When I went to college myself, my understanding of Christian discipleship was strongly shaped by IVP Bible study guides such as *Grow Your Christian Life* and *Patterns for Living with God.* I read and met authors like Paul Little and Francis Schaeffer, who helped me gain a bigger picture of God's purposes in the world. I read foundational books like F. F. Bruce's *The New Testament Documents: Are They Reliable?* and John Stott's *Basic Christianity.* I bought IVP evangelistic booklets and gave them away to my friends. IVP was both stretching and multiplying my faith.

After college, I joined the campus staff of IVCF in New England, and I was thrilled to learn that one of the "perks" of the job was to receive free copies of all newly released IVP books. Those first few years I remember reading every book that IVP published. Now thirty-six years later it is fun to read in *Heart. Soul. Mind. Strength.* some of the stories behind those authors and books!

Several years after my wife, Alice, and I were married, we were invited by IVP to spend a week with Walter and Ingrid Trobisch, authors of several IVP books on dating and marriage relationships. That week of teaching and training enriched our own marriage and led us into a ministry of pre-marital counseling. This in turn led us to develop materials to help prepare couples for marriage.

Linda Doll, a coauthor of this book and my predecessor on IVCF staff in New England, happened to see the purple-inked dittoed handouts we were using and suggested we publish them. They became *A Handbook for Engaged Couples,* which launched Alice's writing career. Linda has always been a step ahead of me, not only on campus staff but in being the director of IVP as well. I am grateful to her for her encouraging role in my life.

The other coauthor of this book, Andy Le Peau, has served IVP with great commitment and distinction for more than thirty years. It is only his personal reticence that has kept his name from appearing more often in this book. Andy has been and continues to be not only a great editorial director but a wise adviser and good friend. We are indebted to Andy for all of his contributions to IVP and especially for this book.

Together Linda and Andy have written a delightful history that captures much of the spirit and sense of God's work in and through IVP. It speaks of our strong sense of mission and our calling to publish books for those "who take their Christianity seriously" and to help our readers better love God and neighbor with "heart, soul, mind and strength."

This book is also full of humor and an honest accounting of some of our foibles and mistakes as well as our successes. But through it all, it is a great tribute to everyone who has worked at IVP, to those authors who have written for us and to the God whom we all serve.

I hope you enjoy reading this anecdotal history of InterVarsity Press just half as much as we have enjoyed living it!

Robert A. Fryling
Publisher
InterVarsity Press

Preface

We, Andy Le Peau and Linda Doll, have worked at InterVarsity Press for a combined total of over sixty-five years. We met in the summer of 1974 when Andy came with a group of new InterVarsity Christian Fellowship campus staff who were taking a tour of IVP as part of New Staff Orientation. We both remember very clearly the banter between us as Andy tried (successfully!) to talk Linda into sending him some extra free IVP books.

We've enjoyed a variety of working relationships over the years. When Andy joined Linda at IVP in 1975, we were peers. When Linda became director of IVP, she was Andy's supervisor. After she stepped down and rejoined the editorial department, Andy became her supervisor. It has been a series of mutually supportive, encouraging and challenging relationships.

In these pages we have tried to preserve not just some of the corporate history but also some of the lore and legend of IVP—the characters who populated the hallways, the comedy that punctuated the years, and the culture that permeated the way we have worked. We are deeply appreciative of those who have helped us recall stories and who have reviewed the manuscript for accuracy, especially Drew Blankman, Steve Board, Cindy Bunch, Sally Sampson Craft, Herb Criley, Jeff Crosby, Bob Fryling, Ralph Gates, Anne Gerth, Jim Hagen, Pete Hammond, Jim Hoover, Keith and Rusty Hunt, Bill McConnell, Mark Noll, Jim Nyquist, Nancy Fox Scott, Jim Sire, Don Stephenson, David Zimmerman and our consummate editor, Al Hsu. Our special thanks also go to Al Fisher, a stalwart of Christian publishing for many years with Baker, P&R and Crossway, who first suggested and encouraged the writing of this book.

Of course we must offer our apologies to the dozens of significant people who have worked at IVP who are not mentioned (or who are barely mentioned) here. There is no way we can provide a full history and mention each of the more than 750 people who have worked at IVP over the decades, but every one has made a contribution to what it is today. Without this wonderful gang of dedicated people, IVP could not have grown and thrived as it has.

We also, of course, take responsibility for this partial collection of facts (and hopefully not much fiction). We have tried to check as many facts as possible. But even the memories of those contributing to it disagree with each other at some points. While we willingly accept responsibility for errors, please read this as anecdotal, not as rigorously historical or comprehensive.

One of the helpful emphases of the postmodern age is the reminder that if we are to look forward, we first have to look back. To know where we are going, we have to know where we have been. To know who we will become, we must know who we were. It is our hope that these pages will offer some modest assistance in reaching that destination.

Linda Doll
Andrew T. Le Peau

Beginnings

The Forties and Fifties

"There is a passion for Christ which it has been given to very few to possess, but which has set those who have it apart for ever from their fellow men. Is not this the quality which separates between Christian and Christian, which marks out some—the rare ones—as beings apart from the rest of us?"

Quiet Time, InterVarsity Press, 1945

The Estrela Penthouse sits on the forty-second floor of the Le Parker Meridian Hotel on West 57th Street in midtown Manhattan. Walls of windows on either end of the room offer picturesque vistas of some of the most famous real estate in the world, overlooking Central Park to the north and the skyline of lower Manhattan to the south. Wednesday, May 26, 2004, had been a mild, misty, overcast day in New York, but the view that evening was still impressive.

In the room were nine or ten round tables, each with a white tablecloth and place settings for six or seven. Some of the best-known people at ABC News had gathered here for a catered buffet meal. Charles Gibson and Diane Sawyer, hosts of *Good Morning America*, were present along with President of ABC News David Westin. Several dozen others from ABC were there, including the anchor of *World News Tonight,* Peter Jennings.

These and a few more were gathered to honor a coworker and friend. In his remarks at the dinner David Westin had said that the world knew their guest of honor as the medical editor of ABC News, "but the employees of ABC News know him as their pastor." Dr. Timothy Johnson had been a familiar face and voice to millions, dispensing medical information over the air for thirty years. This night, these few were honoring their friend for his less familiar side—a man of spiritual depth, passion and compassion.

The impulse for the occasion was the release of Johnson's new book, *Finding God in the Questions,* which had been published just the week before by InterVarsity Press (IVP). Alec Hill, president of IVP's parent organization, InterVarsity Christian Fellowship, opened the evening, followed by IVP Publisher Bob Fryling, who offered a few words about working with Johnson and about IVP. Bob quoted a comment that theologian J. I. Packer, author of *Knowing God,* had made once when Fryling asked how he would characterize IVP and its place in the publishing world. Without hesitation Packer had responded, "Some publishers tell you *what* to believe, and other publishers tell you what you *already* believe, but InterVarsity Press helps you *to* believe."

Afterward Charles Gibson came up to Bob and asked, "What was that quote you mentioned about how IVP is different?" Bob repeated the quote and Gibson responded, "That is a great mission statement for a publisher."

Beginning to Help Readers to Believe

For sixty years the passion of InterVarsity Press has been to help readers grow in their faith in Christ. But IVP had not always fulfilled its calling in such a lofty setting. In fact, this dinner high above New York City was a far cry from the modest beginnings that IVP enjoyed, going back into the 1800s.

There had been considerable evangelical influence in England in the eighteenth and nineteenth centuries. By the late nineteenth century most universities were still Christian, but often in form only, due to modernizing trends. Thus a group of students at Cambridge felt it necessary in 1877 to create the Cambridge Inter-Collegiate Christian Union, or CICCU for short (pronounced "kick-you"), to encourage evangelical faith. Four years later a sister organization, Oxford Inter-Collegiate Christian Union, or OICCU, was founded.

In 1919 sixty members of the two unions gathered in London during an annual "Inter-Varsity" (that is, between universities) sporting match. They decided to meet again, perhaps annually, and to encourage the formation of unions at other universities. By 1928 the Inter-Varsity Fellowship of Evangelical Unions was officially formed, consisting of thirteen university groups.

In 1936 Douglas Johnson, general secretary of the British Inter-Varsity Fellowship (IVF), gave to a fresh graduate from Birmingham University, with no experience in editing or publishing, the job of heading up the literature division. Ronald Inchley combined this part-time role with organizing IVF's extensive city-wide evangelistic campaigns. Inchley inherited a list of about twenty titles, mostly booklets, which had begun to appear in 1928.

A few years later, students in Canada heard about what was happening on campuses across England and invited IVF to send someone to help them start a similar work at their colleges. The students raised enough money for a one-way ticket for Howard Guinness to travel to North America. Guinness was followed by C. Stacey Woods (from Australia), who became general secretary (chief execu-

C. Stacey Woods was the first general secretary of InterVarsity Christian Fellowship/USA.

tive) of the Canadian Inter-Varsity. Not long after, he began receiving requests for help from students in the United States who had heard about what was happening in Canada.

From the very first, when InterVarsity Christian Fellowship (IVCF) began in the United States during the 1939-1940 school year, books were a part of the campus ministry. Initially they were imported from IVF, and the distribution system consisted primarily of IVCF staff members carrying a box or suitcase full of books to sell to students as the staff traveled from campus to campus by bus or car. HIS magazine was also created in 1941 to serve the new campus groups that were forming. With so many Inter-Varsity chapters, the handful of staff could make visits only once every few weeks or months. Thus literature that was left behind became substitute staff for many students, mentoring them in prayer, Bible study, missions, evangelism and leadership.

Almost immediately IVCF felt the need to contextualize literature from England for the North American setting. In 1941 Stacey Woods, who by then was the first head of InterVarsity in the United States with the title General Secretary, wrote to his counterpart in England, Douglas Johnson, about editing the pamphlet *Quiet Time* (a guide to daily devotions) so it would conform more to the colloquial speech of the United States and Canada. Johnson was agreeable as long as the meaning was not changed.

But on December 1, 1941, Johnson wrote with some further thoughts. Apparently permission for a publisher in another country to produce an adaptation had resulted in a disappointing edition. So if any revision was to be made, Johnson asked that all names of original contributors be removed. "Perhaps," he wrote Woods, "you do not realize the amount of horror with which some queer expressions from our friends overseas are received! We should not like any of our more aged contributors to fall dead on the spot if they saw that they had actually said 'Gee, boys, I guess you sure oughta have a Q.T., come along now, yes siree'!" Perhaps these comments reveal something of the (usually friendly) sibling rivalry that was already forming between the two movements as well as British perspectives on America of that era.

As millions of men went to war in Europe and Asia in the early 1940s, many jobs were filled by women, including in the ranks of IVCF campus staff. Stacey Woods recruited Jane Hollingsworth in 1942. A Wheaton College graduate, Jane had also been trained in inductive Bible study at The Biblical Seminary in New York. She brought this passion to her campus work in InterVarsity along with her winsome personality and natural teaching gifts. Woods wanted InterVarsity to be a Bible movement, and

Hollingsworth brought the practical skills needed to make this a reality. Jane emphasized inductive study of large passages of the Bible instead of prooftexting (collecting isolated verses out of context to make a sometimes forced point), a practice very common in the day (as it unfortunately still is now). She also guided students and staff in applying the main truths they discovered to their own lives.

After traveling extensively, visiting students on many campuses, Jane told her boss, "The students want to study the Bible, Stacey, but they don't know how. They need some materials."

"Well, Jane, *write* some!" replied Stacey with his usual bluntness. And so she did.

Jane Hollingsworth (pictured here in an InterVarsity promotional brochure from the early 1940s) led InterVarsity's early emphasis on Bible study among students and wrote IVP's first Bible study guide, *Discovering the Gospel of Mark*.

It wasn't long before IVP published its first inductive Bible study guide in 1943: *Discovering the Gospel of Mark* by Jane Hollingsworth. From the very beginning, three emphases came together in IVP's first home-grown publication: the value of books written by IVCF staff, the importance of Bible study, and the equal worth of books written by men and women—emphases that would sound again and again in the decades to come.

Hollingsworth's book would be followed in the years ahead by other bestselling works from IVCF staff such as Paul Little, Rebecca Manley Pippert, Will Metzger, Robbie Castleman and Don Everts. In addition, other Bible study guides were published in those early years. This trend continued through the publication of the successful LifeGuide Bible Study series launched in the 1980s. Finally, beginning in the forties IVP and IVCF as a whole affirmed the valid role of women as Bible teachers in writing and in speaking. In the sixties and seventies Ada Lum and Barbara Boyd were val-

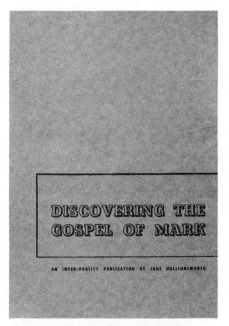

The original cover of *Discovering the Gospel of Mark*. The Bible study guide, published in 1943, was IVP's first publication written and published in the United States. Bible study became a hallmark of IVCF's campus ministry as did Bible study guides for IVP's publishing program.

ued alongside Paul Byer and others as Hollingsworth's successors in Bible study for InterVarsity. Lum especially took up Hollingsworth's mantle as writer of many study guides published by IVP.

Few of the early publications bore the name "InterVarsity Press." The covers of different printings of *Quiet Time* from the late forties read "An Inter-Varsity Booklet" or "An Inter-Varsity Guidebook." The cover of the 1945 printing of *Look at Life with the Apostle Peter,* IVP's second Bible study guide, written by Jane Hollingsworth and Alice Reid, calls it "An Inter-Varsity Publication" but lists "Inter-Varsity Press" as the copyright holder—apparently the first use of the name.

In 1946 Charles J. Miller took on responsibility for publications, ordering books from IVP-UK, printing booklets and HIS reprints. That same year Paul Hopkins, who joined IVCF as its business manager and remained with the movement for four years, had responsibility for public relations, promotion and other business affairs. He also shared responsibility with Miller, including ordering books from England as needed.

In 1947 the board of InterVarsity Christian Fellowship in the U.S.A. determined that the Fellowship should undertake its own deliberate publishing program, replacing the somewhat haphazard activities of the preceding years. That meeting came to be considered the official birth of IVP in the United States. Operating out of the national InterVarsity Christian Fellowship headquarters in Chicago, IVP oversaw the publishing and distribution of books, booklets and Bible study guides in support of the campus work.

After the board decided to pursue publishing seriously, an arrangement was made for Fleming H. Revell, a Christian publisher based in New Jersey, to handle distribution of IVP books to bookstores. The total sum of literature expenditures for the fiscal year 1947-1948 (including for HIS) was $5,317.34, a very modest amount even for that era (equal to $43,989.77 in 2005 inflation-adjusted dollars).

The trickle of IVP titles continued, including *Is Christianity Credible?* by Kenneth Taylor, which was copublished with Moody Press. (Taylor later founded Tyndale House Publishers to produce his *Living Bible.*) *Hymns*, edited by Paul Beckwith, was another early effort.

The publication of *Hymns* in 1947 was to a degree a landmark in American evangelical singing. It set a new standard and the hymnal was adopted by many Christian colleges. It also influenced the content of subsequent church hymnals and unquestionably raised the level of congregational singing. Many hymns now taken for granted in hymnals—"O the Deep, Deep Love of Jesus," "Like a River Glorious," "We Come, O Christ, to Thee" to name only a few out of *many*—were made familiar by *Hymns*.

The singing of hymns with substantive words was a deliberate choice and value that the campus ministry encouraged in contrast to the many frivolous choruses of the day, such as "The Hallelujah Gospel Train." *Hymns* was the primary tool IVCF used to encourage worshipful singing.

The Bayly Era

Joe Bayly, who had joined campus staff in 1944 and had been appointed associate general secretary for the East in 1947, took on leadership of the publishing program in 1951 and functioned as editor of HIS during most of the fifties as well. IVP grew under Bayly's leadership and benefited from his quick wit, keen view of reality, pastoral sensibilities, and exceptional writing and editing skills. As Keith and Gladys Hunt write in their history of InterVarsity Christian Fellowship, "Although his way of meeting editorial deadlines and answering mail often created a frenzy, . . . his large view of God and of student work gave him a strategic ministry through both HIS magazine and the books chosen for InterVarsity Press."

Since IVP had such limited financial resources, however, many books from the British IVF were published in the United States by Eerdmans. In fact, "important as Eerdmans was in promoting American evangelical theologians," wrote historian Mark Noll, "its greater significance for biblical re-

JOSEPH BAYLY

Joseph Bayly was head of IVP (with the title "literature secretary") and was editor of HIS magazine in the 1950s.

Joe Bayly spent sixteen years on the staff of Inter-Varsity Christian Fellowship. He left IVCF in 1960 to form Windward Press, which published a few of his own books as well as Bible study guides by the founders of Neighborhood Bible Studies—former staff members Catherine (Kay) Schell (NCF) and Marilyn Kunz (IVCF). In 1963, Bayly took the post of managing editor at David C. Cook Publishing Company in Elgin, Illinois, eventually becoming its president. He also continued his association with IVCF by serving on the board of trustees until 1982. Bayly died in 1986.

He is probably best known for his writing. He contributed a regular column to *Eternity* magazine, "Out of My Mind," for a quarter century, a column that frequently stirred strong responses from readers—both positive and negative. As long-time *Eternity* editor Russell Hitt said, "Joe wrote [the column] with grace and good humor but he was fearless in confronting evangelicals about questionable practices, false piety, and pompous pretense." He also pioneered Christian satire, a genre not well understood by evangelicals. When he "wrote *The Gospel Blimp,* a parody of mechanical, show-business efforts at evangelism, . . . amazingly, some believers took the *Blimp* to be a manual for evangelism and used it as a study guide!" Bayly also wrote *Psalms of My Life* and *I Saw Gooley Fly,* a portion of which was first published in the February 1954 issue of HIS magazine.

search came through its partnership with British Inter-Varsity." One of the most significant books from Britain, however, was published by IVP in the United States—F. F. Bruce's *The Acts of the Apostles*. The year of publication, 1951, was hailed by New Testament scholar I. Howard Marshall as "the decisive date in the revival of evangelical scholarship in its recognition by other scholars."

The *New Bible Commentary*, however, was too large a project for even Eerdmans to handle on its own in the United States. The British also needed the American, Australian and New Zealand InterVarsity movements to join in and act as distributors. Ronald Inchley in England wrote, "The first printing was 30,000 copies, an unbelievably large quantity for the Press in those days. Of these, 22,000 had been ordered and partly paid for in advance by Eerdmans and the IVCF in the USA."

The early fifties saw changes in sales as well. Revell's pricing and distribution policies complicated the distribution to IVCF students (who were given special discounts). So responsibility for IVP book distribution and HIS magazine circulation returned to the IVCF Chicago office at 1444 N. Astor with the appointment in May 1951 of Keith Hunt as office manager.

Field staff member Paul Carlson began working in the Chicago office August 1, 1954, taking the title publications sales manager, and was assigned to represent both IVF and IVP books to the trade. Paul covered the entire country as IVP's first traveling salesman, trying to interest bookstores—including the one at Knott's Berry Farm—in carrying the books and booklets. He also made IVP's presence known for the first time at the 1956 Christian Booksellers Convention held at the Sherman Hotel in Chicago. That year's catalog included fifty books ranging in price from 15 cents for *Quiet Time* to a hefty $5.95 for the 504-page hardback *A Survey of World Missions* by John Caldwell Thiessen. In addition, twenty-eight booklets were listed, selling for 10 cents each.

Campus staff continued to be instrumental in getting books into the hands of students. With few Christian bookstores in existence and little access through mail order, "staff members carried one suitcase full of literature and another with their clothes. (Barbara Boyd, one of the staff from this era, cites that as the reason her left shoulder is lower than her right.)" As staff met with students for prayer and counsel, it was common practice for students to raise an issue and the staff member to hand them an IVP book to read. The staff would in turn relay to the literature division what was needed on campus—the kind of books and articles other Christian publishers just weren't producing.

One of the most significant publications of the 1950s (and indeed of IVP's entire publishing history) was the booklet *My Heart—Christ's Home* by Robert Boyd Munger, who was pastor of First Presbyterian Church in Berkeley, California, at the time. Originally a sermon given at his church in 1947, its publishing history began in 1951 as an article in the June issue of HIS. It had previously come to the attention of the editors after Munger had preached the message to a group of InterVarsity college students in the Chicago area. The talk had been meticulously transcribed from an old wire recorder (before the development of magnetic tape), and requests to reprint the article were so numerous that IVP decided to publish it at a retail price of 10 cents in 1954. That first year it sold 4,500 copies. The next year it sold over 28,000 copies, and a publishing phenomenon was on its way, eventually selling over ten million copies through IVP and other licensed editions.

Budgets were always tight. In late 1954 Joe Bayly faced the prospect of paying for the upcoming printings of *A Survey of World Missions* by J. C. Thiessen and *The Unchanging Commission* by David Adeney. But neither was there enough money in the account nor did IVP have a line of credit available. To get the cash needed, Bayly sent out a letter on October 11, 1954, "to all staff members asking them to inventory their stock [of IVP books] on hand and as quickly as possible remunerate the Book Department for books which had been sold." He hoped especially that the InterVarsity camps on Catalina Island (Campus by the Sea) and in the Colorado Rockies (Bear Trap Ranch) would be able to come up with the $3,000 in cash owed IVP.

Finances for InterVarsity Press were, even in these early years, handled differently than for the rest of the Fellowship. The board and administration expected that the work of staff members and of national departments of IVCF would be subsidized by national money, that they would not be sustained solely on their own fund raising. As Bayly wrote to Comptroller James McLeish in 1955, "The Board expects [IVP] to be a self-supporting operation in a sense that they do not at present expect any other operation of IVCF, even including the camps, to be self-supporting. . . . The Missionary Department, for instance, is a completely subsidized department." Bayly was very conscious of this expectation and the need to keep increasing sales income to match or better expenses.

With just a handful of employees—and with Bayly's editorial offices in Havertown, Pennsylvania, but other operations being handled in the national office in Chicago—IVP did not always do its work in the most efficient manner. On May 29, 1958, for example, Stacey Woods wrote Bayly that "the British IVF has just about concluded that we in the IVCF-U.S.A. are unbusinesslike and unreliable." IVP-US was in danger of losing all association (and first options) with IVF in England unless promptness and professional dealings were improved. (As members of the International Fellowship of Evangelical Students [IFES], the two publishing houses had an agreement to grant each other first option to publish each other's books, an agreement that is still in effect.) Several key books were lost to Eerdmans because IVP did not exercise its option promptly. Woods said, "The

---

FIRST OPTIONS

A first option is an agreement used among publishers (though now practiced less often) whereby the publisher of a work grants to another publisher or organization an exclusive right to review that work for possible publication in a certain territory or in a certain format. The originating publisher agrees not to offer those publication rights elsewhere until the other party has responded positively or negatively. Usually, however, the option is good only for a specific period of time, such as 60, 90 or 120 days. After that the owner of the work is free to seek to sell it to others.

---

relationship between the British Inter-Varsity Press and the United States InterVarsity Press was . . . 'a rocky road to Dublin' for a number of years."

One book that fell through the cracks was John Stott's new book *Basic Christianity*. Even though IVP had not responded promptly and the book went to Eerdmans, IVP subsequently pleaded that it be allowed to copublish the book. And so an arrangement was made in 1958 whereby IVP would buy copies from Eerdmans who would do the printing—an arrangement that still continues.

Woods attributed Bayly's slow responses to his heavy load and proposed that responsibility for editorial decisions be shared with National Field Secretary Charles Hummel. This began a sequence of discussions guided by Woods that led to Bayly's becoming full-time HIS editor and the formation of a literature committee, with Elizabeth Leake (from McGraw-Hill) being hired as publications secretary, to oversee the management of IVP.

On January 9, 1959, the first meeting of the literature committee was held in Havertown, Pennsylvania. In addition to Woods and Leake, Charlie Hummel and Paul Little were present, with Canadian general secretary H. Wilber Sutherland to join later. They decided that IVCF board members Gordon Van Wylen and Russell Hitt should be asked to serve as ex officio members. The responsibilities of the management committee and the publications secretary were clearly defined, pricing policies were discussed and publication plans were made.

In particular, the group envisioned three groups or series of sixty-four-page pamphlets that authors might see as more feasible to write than full-length works and that readers might see as less time-consuming to read. One series would cover serious intellectual issues of the day, such as the influence of Karl Barth. A second series for freshmen and sophomores would deal with practical issues of the Christian life, such as knowing God's will. A third would consist of Bible study guides.

Over the next several years, books began to emerge as a result of this plan. The first took shape as the IVP series on Contemporary Christian Thought, with volumes from prominent scholars such as *Christianity and Philosophy* by Arthur Holmes (1960), *Emil Brunner* by Paul Jewett (1961), *Christianity and Aesthetics* by Clyde Kilby (1961), *Christianity and Sex* by Stuart Barton Babbage (1963) and two by George Eldon Ladd—*Jesus Christ and History* (1963) and *Rudolf Bultmann* (1964).

The goals of the second series were primarily fulfilled through new booklets, such as *Lost Audience* by Paul Little, published in 1960, and titles from the British IVF. Two Bible study guides were published in 1961—twelve Old Testament character studies by IVCF staff member Marilyn Kunz, under the title *Patterns for Living with God,* and Bible studies by Nurses Christian Fellowship staff called *Standing Orders*. In 1964 a series of daily studies in Luke's Gospel was published as *The Search* by Charles Hummel.

The new literature committee also affirmed that it would be unwise to limit IVP's market exclusively to undergraduates. Otherwise the operation would never end up in the black. It was important that IVP continue to sell both to college students and the general Christian public. And so with all its modest beginnings, IVP grew over the decade of the 1950s from $33,411 in total sales to $89,408, an increase of almost 300 percent.

Creating Core Values

Despite its growth, the Press remained a quintessential shoestring operation, cobbled together with just a few people putting in part-time service, with Mary Ruth Howes doing much of the early editing. The fiscal conservatism that characterized IVP was a necessity, with habits born of years of pinching pennies just to get by and a deep sense of responsibility to steward the resources that had been given sacrificially by donors to the work of InterVarsity. While it may also have resulted partially from the influence of the Depression on those in positions of responsibility at this time, the importance laid on wise stewardship remained for generations of leaders who followed.

More important, however, a tone and mentality had been set for the publishing program. There was a strong emphasis on Scripture, of course, as seen in the Bible studies IVP published, and on quiet time, encapsulated in the pamphlet *Quiet Time,* as the primary spiritual discipline of the Fellowship. This brief collection of advice on daily prayer and Bible reading, written by British campus staff and revised for the American edition, that was published in 1945, eventually sold 900,000 copies.

In addition, IVP (along with IVCF) was heavily influenced by its British roots. Evangelicalism in England did not go through the fundamentalist-modernist controversy as U.S. evangelicalism did, nor did it ever experience a landmark event like the trial of John Scopes in July 1925 for teaching evolution in a public school. In general, British evangelicals, with their strong ties to the established Anglican Church, to Oxford and Cambridge, and to the robust teachings of well-educated Dissenters, did not become anti-intellectual or anticulture in the way their American counterparts tended to. As historian Joel Carpenter writes, "Inter-Varsity brought into the American evangelical domain a number of traits that had developed within the British evangelical student movement. The most important of these, perhaps after the missionary impulse, was a high regard for the life of the mind." As a result InterVarsity did not see itself primarily as an adversary of culture but as a reforming participant in culture.

Likewise, as part of InterVarsity Christian Fellowship, IVP took the university seriously—not as an enemy to be vanquished but as an opportunity to "seek the welfare of the city where I have sent you" (Jer 29:7). InterVarsity was deliberately choosing a different course than separatist Christians of the day who appeared to act as if they should be neither in the world *nor* of the world. As Stacey Woods put it, "Christian students and faculty are a genuine part of the university community with all the privileges, opportunities and responsibilities that the university provides." This holistic approach to the Christian life distinguished InterVarsity from other new Christian movements of the time that were more focused on certain aspects of evangelism or discipleship.

InterVarsity Press, inheriting those sensibilities from England and from the Fellowship as a whole, saw openness to the academic world as a means of bringing minds under the lordship of Christ. IVP was not skeptical of rigorous thinking or nervous about dealing with university ideas and facing intellectual debates head on. While many evangelicals of the day thought that going to the university could lead to losing one's faith, IVP believed that if all truth was God's truth, one need neither be threatened by non-Christian views nor fear the search for truth, wherever it might lead. The world of scholarship, as evidenced by many publications of the forties and fifties coming out of England, was not to be avoided but embraced.

A passion for the Bible, a marked sense of financial stewardship, a missionary impulse, an ardent devotion to Christ, a desire not only to engage culture but to redeem culture, a commitment to the equal value of women and men in Bible teaching, a vision for publishing the writings of InterVarsity staff with a message for the campus as well as the church and world beyond, and a high regard for the life of the mind—these were the values that characterized IVP in its first decades and that would set a pattern for the decades ahead.

The Times They Were A-Changing

The Sixties

"Let us notice carefully that, in saying God is there, we are
saying God exists, and not just talking about the word god,
or the idea god. We are speaking of the proper relationship
to the living God who exists. In order to understand the
problems of our generation, we should be very alive to this
distinction."

FRANCIS A. SCHAEFFER, THE GOD WHO IS THERE, 1968

After Joe Bayly became full-time editor of HIS magazine, the InterVarsity
Press editorial office moved from Havertown, Pennsylvania, to Chicago in
1960. There it became a small part of the larger national IVCF office, located by then at 1519 N. Astor, an old brownstone building one block
from Lakeshore Drive. Ron Ehresman was the one-man order entry/order
fulfillment department. He typed up all the book orders in the morning,
and then went down to the basement, where the books were kept, to pack
and ship all of them in the afternoon. He also did marketing on the side.
The 1960-1961 total number of titles in print (new and previously published) was forty-eight books and twenty booklets.

In InterVarsity, life is sometimes measured by the passing of each Urbana Student Missions Convention, which IVCF usually holds every three years. (The convention takes its name from the location where it was held for many years, the campus of the University of Illinois at Champaign-Urbana.) And IVP played its part in these conventions.

Up until Urbana 61 the Urbana plenary sessions were held in Foellinger Auditorium on the University of Illinois campus. Though IVCF postponed

---

HOW TIMES HAVE CHANGED!

In the early 1960s, the national IVCF headquarters and IVP offices were in a 2 ½-story brownstone house near Lakeshore Drive in Chicago: 1519 North Astor Street. The following are excerpts from *THE IVY, Office Handbook of IVCF* (circa 1964):

Economy of Materials and Equipment: Because this is the Lord's work and we are using the Lord's money, we need to be careful in the use of materials and equipment. Lights should be turned off when not in use, machines kept in good repair and condition, with as little waste as possible. This does not mean, however, that we should go to the other extreme and spend too much time saving paper, etc. Time is as important as money and materials.

Salary: Starting employees will be paid not less than $210 per month.

Insurance: The entire premium for a major medical and life insurance policy is paid for by Inter-Varsity. The amount paid for a single worker for the first year is $4.30 per month; for a married worker, $14.84 per month.

---

the convention a fourth year (from 1960 to 1961) to wait for the new and much larger Assembly Hall, it was delayed by a construction workers' strike. So the Urbana 61 plenary sessions were held in Huff Gym, which could hold more people than the auditorium. Book sales took place in one large room in a dorm along Fourth Street—just several long rows of tables stacked with books. In order to pay, students looked for someone with a cash box.

At Urbana 64, IVCF tried something new—computerized registration! When students mailed in their forms, people in the national office typed in the data and created key punch cards. These were sent to a company in Champaign-Urbana that could process them. But the first thousand key punch cards somehow went astray and never arrived. So the staff members registering the students had to say, "And did you pay us already?" If the students said yes, the staff took their word and said, "Okay," assigning them beds.

In 1964 the new, flying-saucer-shaped Assembly Hall in Urbana (designed, among other purposes, to hold over 16,000 people for the University of Illinois basketball games) held the plenary sessions of the convention. The exhibitor booths for the mission organizations and for book sales

Assembly Hall, Champaign-Urbana, Illinois. Designed to serve as the home of the University of Illinois basketball team, the arena was also the site of plenary sessions for IVCF's Urbana Student Missions Convention from 1964 to 2003.

were located around the perimeter hallways. The doorways (known as "vomitoria") from the auditorium itself into the hallways were numbered, so IVP set up a tent-like IVP Center between vomitoria 16 and 17, calling itself "16½." The book team folks longed for roller skates when they had to go to the opposite side of the huge building.

Turmoil at the Top

In the months leading up to Urbana 64, the upper leadership and board of InterVarsity found itself in turmoil. In March 1964 board president Wallace Erickson hired Richard Wolff as executive assistant to general director

(chief executive) Charles Troutman and as director of InterVarsity Press.
Wolff was

> a bright, aggressive man whose abrasive manner soon alienated almost
> every one in the office. In fairness to Wolff, he was given a bleak picture
> of the state of Inter-Varsity and told by Erickson, who greatly admired
> his gifts, to go in with a strong hand and take care of the situation. . . .
> It soon became obvious to both Troutman and the members of the SAC
> (Staff Advisory Council) that Erickson and Wolff were acting indepen-
> dently of the general director, the staff council, and even the board.
> . . . [Wolff's] seeming disdain for the staff, as well as [for] the history
> and the ethos of the Fellowship, threw the movement into disarray.

This was more than just a power struggle; the values and philosophy of the
Fellowship, including its character as a university movement, were in
jeopardy. Morale was at an all-time low.

In September, Jim Nyquist (who had worked with InterVarsity for his
whole career and was then director of InterVarsity's training camp in the
Rockies, Bear Trap Ranch) stated the conclusions of the SAC in a letter to
board member Roy Horsey, objecting to "Wolff's method of operation, . . .
his intent to change some vital aspects of IVCF's philosophy and . . . his
hand-in-glove relationship with the president of the board." Charles Hummel wrote an eight-page letter to Horsey the same day. Finally, in November, the board requested Wolff's resignation, effective immediately.

As a result of this crisis and the need to fill in the slots vacated by Wolff,
Jim Nyquist was asked not only to be interim director of the central region
and to continue as administrative assistant to the general director but also
to take on supervision of IVP. This last responsibility was handed over to
Nyquist in a rather casual way in the aftermath of Wolff's departure. ("You
might as well take the Press too, Jim.") It would prove to be one of IVP's
most significant turning points, the key to transforming it from a small
publishing operation into a significant voice in the Christian world.

Nyquist had begun his career with InterVarsity in 1949, after serving as
an InterVarsity chapter leader at the University of Minnesota. The standard
staff employment term at the time was three years, but Nyquist refused and
insisted on only a one-year commitment—which turned into a lifetime of

service with IVCF in a variety of capacities. In 1963 he had left the central regional director position to assist Charles Troutman, who was general director of IVCF. When John Alexander became president in 1965, he confirmed that Nyquist's temporary position at IVP should be his primary task.

Jim Nyquist, a man committed to prayer and Scripture, was endowed with seemingly boundless optimism about what God was doing and could do. Those who worked with him admired and respected him greatly. This

THE SWEDE

So much was Jim Nyquist respected at IVP that probably few could imagine what had transpired once in the late 1940s when he had been traveling with Mary Beaton, George Ensworth and other staff to Campus in the Woods in Canada from Minnesota via Michigan. Having a lot of fun with Nyquist's fake Swedish, they decided to tell their overnight hosts in Ontario that he was an IFES (International Fellowship of Evangelical Students) staff worker from Sweden. With his genuine accent (he was still able to speak the native language of his ancestors and relatives), he was so convincing that as the evening progressed, the staff felt embarrassed at the prospect of telling their host that it was all a sham.

The dilemma came to a head at breakfast the next morning when their host asked Nyquist to give thanks. Praying to God with an accent that created a false impression produced an immediate and intense ethical dilemma for Jim as a conscientious Christian. Yet years later, their hosts would ask Mary Beaton how that fine young man from Sweden was doing.

made his annual recitation of " 'Twas the Night Before Christmas" in a thick Swedish accent at the annual IVP office Christmas party even more hilarious. His small stature and his humorous monologue as he donned scarf, hat and mittens (which made it comically difficult for him to turn the pages) only heightened his persona as a jolly elf.

From Chicago to Downers Grove

While the country as a whole was undergoing an upheaval of protests and riots in the late sixties, more changes (of a less violent nature) came to IVP as well. The design of most Christian books in the fifties and sixties was old-fashioned compared with the secular market. Elizabeth Leake (IVP manager from 1959-1964) had begun to call for more attractive cover designs. About that time, Kathy Lay (later Burrows) began to submit designs for booklets while she was still a student at the Illinois Institute of Design. She also agreed with Jim Nyquist that secular books and magazines competed with Christian books whether they liked it or not. And so IVP became a leader in contemporary design, which only some years later came to characterize other Christian publishers.

When Jim Nyquist was given responsibility for the Press, he also carried field responsibilities as interim regional secretary and director of Bear Trap

James Nyquist, here in the early 1970s, worked for IVCF from 1949 to 1985. He was director of InterVarsity Press from 1965 to 1983.

Ranch. Consequently he was given permission in 1966 to open an office in Downers Grove, where he lived, since extensive travel and the long commute each day from his home to the Chicago headquarters was an exhausting arrangement. A three-room office provided space for a portion of the publishing staff. As the work grew, more of the operations were carried out in the Downers Grove office.

Charles O. Miller (not the same Charles J. Miller who handled IV publications in the late forties) worked in production and sales, also living in Downers Grove. Office space was rented on Curtiss Street, just east of Main Street, above a shoe repair shop. Ron Ehresman, Kathy Lay and a couple of others who lived in Chicago came out by train every day. In 1967 HIS also moved to Downers Grove with editor Paul Fromer and other magazine staff.

Since Christian bookstores were few and far between in those days, and since IVP didn't have a very big footprint in those that did exist, IVP established several "Permanent Book Tables" (PBT) to get books into the hands of readers wherever possible. PBT operators were individuals (usually associated with the campus work) who had no storefront but operated out of their garages, basements and the trunks of their cars. In order to make books available to students, especially at conferences, special discounts were given to these graduates who helped the staff by ordering books, setting them up and handling book sales during intercollegiate events. This system was highly successful for many years. The star PBT operator of the era was Walter Seigfried in Pittsburgh, who in the 1960s sold more IVP books per year than any other PBT and more than most bookstores.

Once, a PBT operator was in a bookstore and met a woman he knew, who was shopping there. Always willing to help, he told her, "Hey, don't pay full price for that book here in the store; I can sell it to you at a discount!" PBTs were not intended to compete with bookstores, however! The store manager overheard the conversation, and IVP's marketing team had some work to do to repair relations with the bookstore.

Seeing the need to keep IVCF alumni in touch with new releases of IVP, the always entrepreneurial Nyquist launched Press-O-Matic (later called the IVP Book Club) in 1966. Those few hundred who first signed up for the program would automatically receive all new IVP books unless they sent in a postcard declining the offer. What started as a mimeographed listing of books without photos of covers evolved over the decades into a major full-color brochure that quickly got new books into the hands of avid readers.

The year 1966 also brought the landmark publication of *How to Give Away Your Faith* by IVCF staff member Paul Little. It remained among IVP's top-selling books for decades, selling over 900,000 copies. The manuscript had been tediously put together from old-fashioned reel-to-reel tapes recorded during Paul's lectures at Wheaton College. The entire process took months, but it soon became clear that it was worth the struggle! The book helped establish IVP as a significant publisher not only for students but for the wider church.

This raised a question for some within InterVarsity, however. "Shouldn't

InterVarsity Press publish books just for students? After all, InterVarsity is a student ministry." As IVP grew, the range of topics it addressed grew as well. And so did the North American student population—changing from mostly white kids in ivy-covered dorms to a diverse group from all racial and ethnic backgrounds, many of them commuters, many married and with children, many returning to study at an older age. The issue was discussed, and the IVCF board made a statement on July 29, 1966, recognizing that distribution of IVP products "to every segment of society is appropriate, provided such distribution does not hinder the primary ministry to IVCF constituents." This became a significant touchstone for future development.

By the next year, the little office on Curtiss Street wasn't big enough. So Jim Nyquist rented a white house with blue gingerbread trim on Warren Street, facing the tracks, beside the Moose Hall. (The house no longer ex-

Soon after Urbana 67, InterVarsity Press occupied this white house on Warren St., Downers Grove, Illinois, facing the Burlington-Northern railroad tracks.

ists.) IVP moved there soon after Urbana 67. The elderly occupants were gone, but the furniture remained. An orange dinette booth was moved from the kitchen to the basement where the typesetting machines were located. The typesetters had to cope with mushrooms growing in the musty carpet. One day the staff "ordered in" from nearby Downers Grove Chop Suey. They spread out beyond the dinette set—and spilled soy sauce into the typesetting equipment!

As IVP sales increased, business functions gradually moved out of 1519 North Astor Street (IVCF headquarters). With the move of the Chicago office to Madison, Wisconsin, in 1969, almost all of the publishing functions were consolidated in Downers Grove. IVP had previously contracted for Moody Press to do its warehousing and shipping. Moody's head, Harold Shaw, was an IVCF board member who helped Jim Nyquist learn the publishing ropes. Being in two locations became awkward when invoicing moved from Chicago to Downers Grove.

As a result, the books were moved to Downers Grove as well—to a former garage behind the Grant Dixon Real Estate office, just across the alley from the little white house on Warren Street. This Quonset-hut-shaped building became the warehouse. When it was necessary to communicate

IVP AND HAROLD SHAW PUBLISHERS

The connections between Harold Shaw Publishers and IVP began when Harold was on the IVCF board, but they didn't stop there. Northcote Deck was the father of Harold's wife, Luci. A missionary surgeon in the Solomon Islands, Deck was a plenary speaker at Urbana 48 and Urbana 51 and a member of the IVCF board in the 1950s. He also wrote a booklet for IVP titled *The War That Never Ends,* based on a 1949 HIS magazine article. HIS also published poetry by his daughter Luci in the sixties and seventies, beginning in 1965 with her first published poems outside of Wheaton College periodicals, a thrill she still remembers.

In the late 1960s, Harold Shaw, serving as business manager for Tyndale House Publishers, along with Luci began Harold Shaw Publishers (HSP), focusing on fiction, poetry, Bible studies and nonfiction. In 1984, Harold Shaw contracted cancer, dying a year later. Luci assumed responsibilities as president of HSP until she sold the business in 1990 to Steve Board, former editor of HIS magazine.

Steve, in turn, sold HSP in 2000 to WaterBrook Press in Colorado Springs, where it operates as one of their imprints, Shaw Books. For its first five years at WaterBrook, Shaw was under the editorial direction of Elisa Fryling Stanford, daughter of IVP publisher Bob Fryling. In 2005, exactly forty years after her first poems were published in HIS magazine, Luci Shaw's first IVP book was published, *The Crime of Living Cautiously.*

between the two buildings, the staff used a walkie-talkie on the wall. Various people took two-hour shifts answering the phone (then shouting up the stairs, "Ellie, it's for you"). When the call was for someone in the warehouse, the person who answered the phone in the white house would say, "Could you call back, please, and I won't answer, and after the fourth ring the warehouse will pick it up." Not sophisticated, but it worked.

Jim Nyquist was also responsible for spearheading the editorial process

HIS MAGAZINE

HIS magazine was started by IVCF in the fall of 1941 to offer students a philosophy of ministry on campus and to connect the new network of InterVarsity chapters right from the start. HIS was always a separate entity from InterVarsity Press, even though their lives intertwined over the years. They occupied the same offices but were financially and editorially distinct. Only in the 1950s did editorial responsibility overlap when Joe Bayly was both literature secretary, responsible for IVP, and editor of HIS.

Early editors include some well-known names like Robert Walker (1942-1944, who later started *Christian Life* magazine), Kenneth Taylor (1944-1946, of *Living Bible* fame), Virginia Lowell Grabill (1947-1951), Wilbur M. Smith (part time 1948-1949 while also teaching at Fuller), Stacey Woods (also part time 1949-1952) and, of course, Joseph Bayly (1952-1960, later president of David C. Cook). The copyright of the name HIS was successfully defended legally at least once, when a magazine of the same name appeared on newsstands with other sexy periodicals!

Virginia Krauss (later Hearn) was assistant editor, and Gordon Stromberg was the art editor during the magazine's first years in Chicago. HIS was part of life in the white house in the 1960s. Kathy Lay worked in the white house even before she was married to Tom Burrows, commuting from Chicago. Paul Fromer, editor of HIS from 1960-1971, put plywood across the bathtub in the bathroom of HIS's quarters so that manuscripts and magazines could be stacked high in that space.

In 1971 Steve Board, former campus staff in Chicago, became editor of HIS magazine for four years following Paul Fromer. When he left in 1974 to become editor of *Eternity* magazine, HIS ran an editorial titled "Board with Eternity." After serving in an "acting" capacity for a year, Linda Doll was HIS editor from 1976 until 1983, when David Neff took charge until he accepted an editorial position at *Christianity Today*. Verne Becker then stepped into David's shoes in 1985.

and acquired the manuscripts. Sylvia Clark and Claire Alexander did freelance editing. Carol Adeney created the book *This Morning with God* from daily sets of questions first published in HIS. IVP had no full-time editors.

Eventually the basement furnace room in the white house functioned as the darkroom for Mickey Moore, HIS art editor, as well as the lunchroom. Wilma Holmes, manager of the warehouse, mixed up lots of leftover paint and brightened it up. Someone sewed a colorful curtain for the doorway. At that time, IVCF had an "evangelistic coffee house" in downtown Chicago with the name *The Alternative.* John Rhine, who worked in production at IVP, put a sign above the IVP furnace room/lunchroom door: *"The Last Alternative. Abandon hope, all ye who enter here."*

A Critical Year

The year 1968 was an eventful one for the nation, beginning with the Tet Offensive in Vietnam in January, followed by President Johnson's announcement he would not run for reelection, the assassinations of Dr. Martin Luther King Jr. in March and Robert F. Kennedy in June, the "Prague Spring" crushed by Soviet tanks in August, the tumultuous Democratic National Convention in Chicago a week later, the November election of Richard Nixon, and the first manned orbit of the moon by the Apollo 8 astronauts in December.

Likewise, the year was an eventful one for InterVarsity Press, though not for world-shaking reasons. Relations with IVF in England were improving substantially as IVP-US was able to adequately market books in the United States and responded more quickly to options for acquiring new books from England. Jim Nyquist said:

> The name Inter-Varsity Press [then written with a hyphen] was adopted by us in the early 1960s, as I recall. Ronald Inchley, the Inter-Varsity Fellowship publisher in London, approached me about changing their name from IVF Publications to IVP. This was heartily endorsed and the change was made in 1968; joint printing became simpler and the common name was beneficial on both sides of the Atlantic.

Jim Nyquist hired Jim Sire as IVP's first full-time editor, who began work June 1, 1968. *How to Give Away Your Faith* had sold well enough to allow

IVP to add this position. Sire had earned his Ph.D. at the University of Missouri and had taught English at Nebraska Wesleyan, where he had also been on the InterVarsity local committee, helping to raise support for campus staff. Sire was a bearded academic, a specialist in Milton who never quite lost his intellectual elitism. Soon, however, he learned to be a generalist as manuscripts came his way dealing with a broad range of disciplines including philosophy, art, theology, history and more. Sire knew little of publishing, but he had enough confidence to take on the role as editor, having successfully contracted to write one academic book before coming

SCHAEFFER AND WHEATON

In 1965 Francis Schaeffer created a stir when he gave a series of lectures at Wheaton College. Dressed in knickers, hiking boots, a turtleneck sweater and Swiss jacket, speaking with a raspy voice of philosophical and spiritual realities, Schaeffer produced cognitive dissonance at this center of mid-century evangelicalism in Illinois. "Students were fighting to show films like *Bambi,* while Francis was talking about the films of Bergman and Fellini. Administrators were censoring existential themes out of student publications while Francis was discussing Camus, Sartre, and Heidegger. He quoted Dylan Thomas, knew the artwork of Salvador Dali, listened to the music of the Beatles and John Cage." These talks later formed the core of the book published under the title *The God Who Is There.*

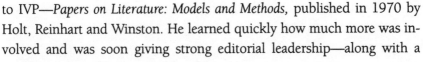

to IVP—*Papers on Literature: Models and Methods,* published in 1970 by Holt, Reinhart and Winston. He learned quickly how much more was involved and was soon giving strong editorial leadership—along with a goodly portion of humor and laughter to any conversation.

Gordon Lewis, professor at Denver Conservative Baptist Seminary, also had a book published in 1970—this one by IVP—*Decide for Yourself,* a theological workbook. He told Sire he thought he, Gordon, would put his children through college on the royalties of that book. "Don't burden me with that," Sire told him. "But I think I will be able to do that with the royalties from *my* book." As it turned out, Lewis's book eventually sold over 100,000 copies. Sire's sold less than a thousand. Sire concluded at this point that God wanted him to edit books, not to write them.

When Sire came to IVP, the kitchen became his office. Jim Nyquist had the back bedroom. The living room held several desks: Dot Bowman (Jim Nyquist's secretary), Wynema Marlatte (Paul Former's secretary hired in January 1968), Anne Clement and later Ellie Meyer, doing HIS circulation, and a couple others. Marj Sire, at home with small children, started working for IVP in August of that year, tearing apart sales invoices. Later she did typesetting in the evenings.

The year 1968 was also the year that IVP began publishing Francis Schaeffer's works. Schaeffer was a Presbyterian pastor who went to Europe as a missionary in the late 1940s, founding L'Abri Fellowship in 1955.

> Eventually young people from all over the globe began streaming up to the Schaeffers' alpine home in an obscure part of Switzerland, a pilgrimage perhaps unique in the history of evangelicalism. By word of mouth the news had spread to college and university students in a rapidly globalizing world that there was a place in the Alps where one could get honest answers to life's deepest questions.

Schaeffer's work as an apologist and his role as a prophet of evangelicalism grew.

Jim Nyquist obtained rights for Schaeffer's first two books, *The God Who Is There* from Hodder and Stoughton in England and *Escape from Reason* from IVP-UK. As Jim Sire wrote:

> *Escape from Reason* would have been published first, but its delivery from the British printer was postponed by a strike on the St. Lawrence Seaway. *The God Who Is There* was being printed in the United States, the result being that both books were released in the fall of 1968, just a few days before Schaeffer gave [a series of] lectures at Wheaton College.

These books raised IVP's profile even further.

One of Jim Sire's first acts as editor at IVP was to proofread the already printed back cover of *The God Who Is There*. When he laid the large four-up cover sheet on the musty basement floor, he noticed that the last name of the French intellectual Jean-Paul Sartre was spelled without the second *r*. Ten thousand covers had to be trashed and reprinted with the correct spelling at a time when finances were exceptionally tight. But how could a publisher of books for university students launch a major title on the intellectual forces shaping the era with such a glaring error? The commitment to quality won over financial considerations, as strong as they were, even in these early years.

In Sire's first weeks he also supported a plan to place a classified ad for

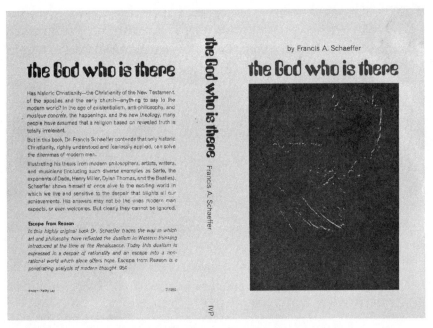

The original cover of Francis Schaeffer's *The God Who Is There*, published by IVP in 1968, with Sartre's name on the back lacking the second *r*.

Escape from Reason in the *Chicago Tribune*. The seven-line ad appeared on page 24 of section 1A of the Sunday, July 28, 1968, edition. "ESCAPE FROM REASON," it read, "by Dr. Francis Schaeffer. A perceptive analysis of Western man's new mysticisms—aesthetic, religious, existential, sexual. Send $1.00."

Six weeks later Nyquist jotted a note to Sire, "Would you please find out what response we got to *Escape from Reason* Tribune want ad?"

Sire wrote back, "Sure. 1 purchase. Experiment a success. We'll never do that again."

Jim Sire also played a major part in turning Schaeffer's lectures into books, thus expanding Schaeffer's influence. The first of these was *Death in the City*, based on those 1968 Wheaton College lectures given September 30 to October 4, and published in 1969. After hearing the lectures, Sire said to Nyquist, "I don't think this is a book, but if it becomes one, we've got a title for it," since at the end Schaeffer yelled his closing words, "There's death in the city. There's death in the city. There's death in the city." Of course it proved to be not only a title but a book that became another IVP bestseller.

Students at Harvard and other colleges would gather to listen to the cassette tapes of lectures Dr. Schaeffer had given at L'Abri in Switzerland. In New England, everyone knew the name of Schaeffer beer. When Francis Schaeffer came to Boston to speak, lapel buttons appeared on campus at MIT, Wellesley, Harvard and so on, proclaiming, "Schaeffer is not a beer." Inquirers were invited to the lectures, which were aimed at skeptics and seekers.

Know Why You Believe by Paul Little was also published in 1968 and immediately became another top-selling book—even though it was simultaneously being published by Scripture Press. This unintentional copublishing arrangement arose when Paul Little, somewhat unfamiliar with the world of publishing at the time, made an agreement for the book to be published with Scripture Press in 1967 as part of a curriculum package. Jim Nyquist's understanding was that it would be sold for just one year, after which IVP would take it on. But Scripture Press was under the impression from the author that they would be able to continue publishing the book after the first year. As a result, a gentleman's agreement was made whereby both publishers would continue to produce it—an arrangement that continues, several editions later, to this day.

During this time, "Gordon Van Wylen, dean of engineering at the University of Michigan in Ann Arbor, had been discussing with Regional Director Keith Hunt the idea of a campus-related Christian bookstore that would serve as a place to disseminate helpful Christian literature and initiate evangelistic conversations." Van Wylen led an Ann Arbor committee in raising $12,000 for the project. With the encouragement of Jim Nyquist and under his supervision, the first Logos Bookstore in the country was opened near the campus on July 15, 1968.

Nyquist hired Jim Wilson (who had been a bookstore manager on the East Coast) to head up the store. Jim Carlson, who had been on InterVarsity campus staff and was just finishing his studies at Gordon-Conwell Theological Seminary in Massachusetts, called Nyquist to see if he might know about any job opportunities. When Nyquist mentioned the bookstore, Carlson was immediately interested and was soon hired as the business manager.

Early on, however, Jim Wilson said that he didn't want to have any book in the bookstore that he could not personally endorse. Nyquist felt that such a policy wouldn't make for a successful bookstore in a university community. So Jim Wilson left the store and Jim Carlson became the overall manager.

When the store opened, a prayer request was placed in *The Intercessor,* IVCF's monthly prayer guide sent to supporters, regarding the need for funding this new venture. As a result, people in other parts of the country asked about starting similar stores, and by 1970 there were five Logos Bookstores around the country, opened on a franchise basis. IVP eventually owned two other stores as well, one in Minnesota and one in Chicago.

The pivotal year of 1968 neared its end. In November Linda Doll moved from Boston to join the staff of InterVarsity Press. She had worked on campus staff since 1961 in New England. Before Urbana 67 she traveled to the

JIM CARLSON

After years of building up the Logos chain, Jim Carlson saw the need for a distributor to supply books from many publishers to Christian retail stores. In this way stores would be saved the trouble of ordering from dozens of different publishers and could place a single order for most of their needs. While several major distributors served the general book trade in this way, none was focused on the Christian market. So in the early 1980s Carlson founded Spring Arbor Distributors in Belleville, Michigan, which grew rapidly into the largest Christian book distributor in the country. In 1997 Ingram Book Group, the largest book distributor in the country overall, bought Spring Arbor and folded it into its operations.

Midwest to assist with preparations for the convention and was assigned to help Jim Nyquist with the bookselling operation for a couple weeks.

During that time Nyquist asked her to "smooth out and improve" some material for a book that was soon to be published. When she did so, he looked at it and responded, "When are you going to come work with us at IVP?" Though she was flattered, she didn't think he was serious. After the convention, though, he repeated the offer.

By the summer of 1968, funds for campus staff in New England were tight. Linda's boss, Harold Burkhart, told her and the team that cuts were likely. Remembering Jim Nyquist's offer, she mentioned it to Harold. He and Nyquist talked, and in November she drove her Volkswagen Beetle to Downers Grove, where Jim Sire and Ron Ehresman helped her unload it. She began by copyediting under Jim Sire's direction and later also worked in campus sales to InterVarsity chapters.

Less garrulous than Sire and less assertive than Kathy Lay, Linda was sometimes shocked in her early days at IVP by the rather direct exchanges that took place between these two coworkers as they discussed (to her ears, argued over) cover designs. Just as shocking, however, was how much they continued to enjoy working with each other. Apparently one could disagree without being disagreeable. This was a revelation to her.

Up to Date

Business was growing so fast for IVP that it was hard to keep up. At one point the distribution center was three weeks behind, stacked high with books that needed packing and invoices that needed picking. All employees were asked to take a turn at packing books to help catch up. The continued shoestring nature of the operation was also typified by the fact that Sire had to get permission from Nyquist to make long-distance phone calls.

The Christian Booksellers Association (CBA) Convention was smaller in those days too. The booths were simpler and less splendid than they became in later decades. A table with books and a few signs were sufficient for many exhibitors in contrast to the six-figure booths many publishers would eventually sport. IVP, of course, was budget-conscious. In 1969, when the convention was in Cincinnati, production manager Charles Miller and new business manager Herb Criley loaded all the display materials into a trailer that they hitched to a station wagon.

Driving merrily to Cincinnati, they went over a railroad track and felt something snap. They looked back. To their horror, the trailer had detached and was following them at top speed! Herb yelled, "Hit it, Charles—it's gaining on us!" The trailer soon veered off into a cornfield. Charles and Herb rescued the remnants of the trailer and the display, took a short nap, started driving again at 4 a.m., and had the booth set up on the convention floor by starting time at 11 a.m.

IVP urged campus staff teams in various parts of the country to designate certain staff as Staff Lit Specialists. The Press encouraged each InterVarsity chapter to designate a Student Lit Chairman. Ron Ehresman compiled the *Lit Chairman's Handbook* for use in training students to help their chapters use books for evangelism and discipleship.

A popular medium of the day was the "underground newspaper." Anything that looked as though it was connected to "the establishment" would cause an immediate loss of credibility on campus. So IVP followed suit and printed (on newsprint) *The (Lit) Pusher* to give to chapter lit chairmen. IVP's underground newspaper contained stories and ideas about how literature could be used for campus outreach. Three "lit tapes" were also made—training cassettes to mail to the student and staff lit specialists. These were produced in the basement office at the white house facing the tracks in Downers Grove. A $40 cassette recorder was used, recording in low-tech fashion, so occasionally a train going by across the street could be heard on the tape.

In addition IVP published several issues of another newspaper-style piece titled *The Fish,* which was written for non-Christians, some of its articles being reprinted from Colorado's *The Boulder Fish.* The idea was for InterVarsity students to buy it in bulk and distribute it on campus. *The Fish* attempted to intrigue readers with the gospel and with who Jesus really was.

In the late sixties with Jim Nyquist's willingness to continue venturing into new arenas, IVP began producing music long before the Christian music industry became so prominent. InterVarsity Records (IVR) released 33-1/3 rpm LP records. The half dozen albums produced included three by singer Linda Rich, two collections of hymns and one by Jonathan (Guest) and Charles (Hess), *Another Week to Go,* which included a song titled "Jesus Was a Pretty Good Guy." Predictably, some took offense at this title and complained. If they had listened to the song—the next line is "so they tell me," and the singer's position becomes clear as the song goes along—they might have appreciated the intent behind the unsettling words. Sales of the records were modest. Feeling they were not central to

JIM NYQUIST

Jim Nyquist served in many capacities for IVCF before taking on InterVarsity Press. He was a regional director beginning in 1950 and camp director at Campus in the Woods north of Toronto (1952-1957) and Bear Trap Ranch just west of Colorado Springs (1958-1967). In 1963 he left his position as director of the Central Region to assist Charles Troutman, general director of IVCF. Jim served as director of IVP (along with other assignments) from late 1964 till 1983, when, as a vice president, he supervised both the literature division and all departments in the national office in Madison, other than the field, until he was retired in 1985.

Jim was the person who turned IVP from a small literature distribution service to a major evangelical publisher with an impact many times its size. Nyquist had an entrepreneurial side as he helped many new ventures get under way. He watched over not only IVP and HIS but also these related ministries:

- Bible and Life training (a series of discipleship training weekends for students)
- Logos Bookstores
- Schloss Mittersill bookkeeping (the IFES-related castle in Austria with training programs for students and others)
- Ediciones Certeza (an imprint of books produced and originating in Argentina for the IFES movements in Latin America, which IVP managed for a few years till it could be taken back to Argentina and overseen by an international committee)
- IVP's damaged and surplus books program, providing free books for IFES sister movements in countries with minimal economic resources

In 1984 Nyquist also helped Nurses Christian Fellowship launch a new magazine, *Journal of Christian Nursing* (or *JCN*). Kathy Lay Burrows, then art director for IVP, took on its design, and its first editor, Ramona Cass, had her office at IVP's Main Street location in Downers Grove.

IVP's mission, Jim Nyquist decided the program should be dropped.

IVP customarily had a weekly office/prayer meeting in the basement of the white house. Leadership was rotated. Warehouse manager Roosevelt Davis, an African American Christian, led stirring sessions, teaching folks to "amen" and nod in affirmation of the truths he spoke about.

From IVP's inception, all of its financial activity was handled by the accounting department of the national office. Because they also were understaffed and overworked, IVP wouldn't know whether it was profitable until six months after the accounting books were closed! Jim Nyquist, without any other financial information, was making decisions merely on the basis of how much money IVP had in its bank account—the only figures he had available to him. Charles Miller knew the Press didn't have enough cash to pay its print bills, and so he kept them in a drawer in his house, unpaid—until Nyquist discovered what was happening! Finally, by the late 1960s, the national office granted permission for IVP to keep its own accounting so it could manage its resources better.

This major change came about when Herb Criley joined IVP in January 1969 as business manager, having been the manager for the national Inter-Varsity office in Chicago. He was able to get IVP's accounts in order and give Nyquist the data needed to make informed decisions.

In 1969-1970 Criley also advised even more emphasis on the book club, Press-O-Matic, which had been growing steadily, to help with income. So Jim Nyquist brought in Al Youngren as a marketing consultant, and the book club successfully expanded, eventually reaching almost fifteen thousand members. In the 1970s it became a foundation stone for growth. With a small sales and marketing team, responsibility for selecting titles and writing all the promotional copy for the club fell to Jim Sire. Most new books sold an initial one to two thousand copies through the club to some of the most important opinion leaders in the church, who would then recommend the book to others. This seeding of the market was extremely effective in creating strong word-of-mouth promotion that outstripped IVP's financial ability to advertise. (Press-O-Matic was renamed the IVP Book Club in 1990 and still operates successfully with about nine thousand members. Because IVP now publishes about a hundred books each year, not all are offered automatically to members.)

During the 1960s, sales grew over 600 percent, spurred by the success of books from Paul Little and Francis Schaeffer as well as by the growth of the Jesus People movement, which paralleled the rise of political activism during that period. Jim Nyquist kept IVP in the greater Chicago area when the national office moved to Wisconsin, and he kept financial reporting within IVP. More important, he had charted the course for even further growth in the coming years by bringing together a strong team of people in editorial, marketing, design, production and finance that would increase IVP's impact on the church worldwide.

Expansion and Growth

The Seventies

IVP

"Christians and non-Christians have something in common: We're both uptight about evangelism."

REBECCA MANLEY PIPPERT,
OUT OF THE SALTSHAKER AND INTO THE WORLD, 1979

As the new decade opened, evangelical Christianity was on the rise in the United States. Billy Graham was nearing the peak of his influence. The spirit of the Jesus People movement, begun in 1967 in San Francisco, was spreading to other parts of the country. Hal Lindsey's book on end times, *The Late Great Planet Earth,* published in May 1970, was recognized by the *New York Times* as the number one nonfiction bestseller of the decade. Campus Crusade for Christ held a massive rally in the Cotton Bowl in Dallas, called Explo '72, drawing eighty thousand people and earning the cover story on *Life* magazine. Richard Ostling noted, "During the 1970s evangelical programs on television proliferated, reaching an audience of more than 20 million."

New Christian bookstores were now opening at a great rate as this new surge of activity pulsed through the country. In 1961 the Christian Booksellers Association had a membership of 830; by 1975 attendance at the CBA convention broke 5,000 for the first time. IVP sales to Christian bookstores grew along with them, rising 75 percent in 1969 and another 33 percent in 1970.

To capitalize on this growth area, marketing consultant Al Youngren designed a floor rack for books and in 1971 launched the IVP Rack Program. Stores loved the black wire fixture. The marketing and sales team also created triangular "mobiles" that could hang from the store ceiling and large posters that stood atop The Rack, saying "Grow Your Mind." With this program it was not necessary to promote and advertise every book individually. IVP could stretch its meager marketing dollars effectively by promoting the whole line of books at once. The Rack proved extremely successful in giving dozens of IVP books face-out exposure, rather than the more typical spine-out exposure. Hundreds of thousands of books have been sold over the decades through this program, and The Rack became an object of envy for other publishers who craved such effective in-store merchandising for themselves—and who eventually produced similar racks of their own.

A few years later, large photos of IVP's bestselling authors (John Stott, Rebecca Manley Pippert, Francis Schaeffer and Paul Little) were added on top of The Rack. IVP also created other in-store fixtures such as shelf displays, a booklet rack and cardboard counter displays for just one book—anything to catch consumers' attention.

The Press also caught CBA's attention the year the team took a button machine along. It was a hand-powered clamp that pressed together a metal backing with a pin in it, some photo or piece or art in the middle, and a plastic circle that formed the front of the button. Yes, it was low-tech, but when IVP offered to take Polaroid photos of people and put them in a button, folks at CBA flocked to the booth! And they wore their buttons proudly.

Another creative marketing effort occurred at the CBA convention held in Denver in 1971. Al Youngren and others set up a bus tour that would take interested bookstore people up into the mountains high above Colorado Springs to gorgeous Bear Trap Ranch, an InterVarsity campground at a 9,000 ft. elevation, where they would have a meal amidst the beauty of Colorado's forests and streams. Youngren hired several school buses and drivers for the trip. But one bus slipped slightly over the edge on the steep, rail-less road and got stuck! The driver declared that he was through and that someone else could drive it back down the mountain. Patience and good humor wore thin as new arrangements took time and folks missed all the evening sessions at the convention.

Consolidating Locations

As IVP outgrew the little white house, the office space on Curtiss Street was rerented as was additional warehouse space near Walnut Street in Downers Grove. Charles Miller had his office at his home. So IVP was in five separate locations for a year or two.

The situation obviously needed attention, so IVP purchased the former Buick dealership at 5206 Main Street. The move took place in early 1971,

InterVarsity Press moved its offices and distribution to 5206 Main St., Downers Grove, Illinois, in early 1971. It attempted to deal with the showroom windows of the former Buick dealership by lining them with brown paper.

soon after Urbana 70, and was an adventure. Wynema Marlatte and others spent hours scrubbing greasy windows. Furniture, equipment and supplies were carried to the second floor in the huge car-sized elevator (cars had been repaired on the second floor), even as carpenters, electricians and phone installers did their work. The upstairs was partially converted to offices with the rest set aside for storage. The entire ground floor was devoted to warehousing and shipping. With the automobile grease quotient reduced, the building served IVP for the next twenty-four years.

One problem was what to do with the large showroom windows that wrapped around the corner of building. These had worked well for a car dealership, but IVP needed the space for storage. It wouldn't look good to have stacks of boxes exposed to the street, so the large windows were lined with huge sheets of brown paper. This succeeded in blocking the view of pedestrians so they couldn't look inside, but they actually became even more curious about what kind of publishing operation was going on when they saw, emblazed on the windows, the words, "HIS magazine." Many residents of Downers Grove were scandalized with the thought that a racy men's magazine might be in production right in the middle of their quiet, conservative village!

To offset this misimpression, copies of some of IVP's latest books were later placed on display in one of the windows. Unfortunately, copies of Walter Trobisch's new books *Love Is a Feeling to Be Learned* and *My Wife Made Me a Polygamist* did little to correct mistaken notions.

At this time Linda Doll served as the campus liaison (among other duties). She took collect calls one evening a week, at home, 7-11 p.m. Central

A BUILDING WITH A HISTORY

An auditorium was originally built on the site of the 5206 Main Street building in 1890 by D. W. Crescy, a politician who once pulled 400,000 votes to become an elector for Grover Cleveland. Townspeople gathered here to see plays, attend revival meetings and hold school suppers. After the building burned down, it was replaced with a brick structure that became a plumbing and garage service operated by Herbert and Frank Hawkins. The brothers added a third floor in the late 1920s or early 1930s, but a fire destroyed it and it was removed.

During the Depression, the Hawkins brothers were forced to let the building go, and it was purchased in 1938 by Floyd "Biff" Baughman for his Buick and Pontiac dealership. Thirty-three years later IVP rented the building with an option to buy, an option it exercised a few years after that.

Standard Time, from the student literature chairmen of InterVarsity chapters. They ordered books or asked for advice on setting up a good campus booktable. Once, sound asleep, Linda got a call at 1 a.m. from a student eager to place an order. She thought, *At 1:00? Well, he's probably in California and it's only 11:00 there.* So she asked where he was from—and he told her he was from Yale!

Shortly after moving into the Main St. offices in 1971, IVP employees greet designer (and photographer) Kathy Burrows in the main office hallway. Clockwise from lower left: Linda Doll (editorial and campus sales), Wilma Holmes (distribution), Nora Holmes (typesetting), John Rhine (production), Jim Nyquist (director), Jock Binnie (sales), Jim Sire (editorial), Herb Criley (business), Charles Miller (production).

"How come you're calling at 2 a.m. your time?" she asked.

His typical-student reply: "Well, because I was taking a study break . . ."

At times IVP's spirit of fiscal responsibility reached unprecedented heights. When new catalogs and order forms were printed, Wilma Holmes, then manager of distribution, would throw away the old ones. When Charles Miller saw them in the dumpster, however, he would retrieve them

STEVE BOARD

Steve Board, editor of HIS in the early seventies, was known for his dry and imaginative wit. He particularly enjoyed collecting stationery from various institutions, like the White House, photocopying the letterhead onto a fresh sheet of paper and then writing his own fictitious missives to friends or officemates. Several of these inventive creations made their way onto the office bulletin board for all to enjoy.

One day Board, at the peak of his powers, realized that HIS had inadvertently republished an article without getting proper permission. In addition, he discovered that HIS had somehow actually given permission to *Campus Life* magazine to reprint it as well, even though HIS had no right to do so. Immediately a plan was born in his mind.

He created fake stationery from the law firm of "Abercrombie & Fitch, Attorneys at Law," and sent a letter to his friends at *Campus Life,* written in his best lawyer-eze. The letter sternly informed *Campus Life* that a lawsuit was being brought against it for copyright infringement. The letter also referenced HIS magazine, with a notation that a carbon copy had been sent to HIS as well.

After mailing the letter, Steve kept waiting for a phone call from Wheaton. He asked Barb Sroka, his assistant editor, to be sure to forward the call to him as soon as it came in. He was sure that the notation of a carbon copy to HIS and the name of the law firm would be dead giveaways as to who was really behind the letter. But Abercrombie and Fitch was not as well known nationally for their apparel as they are today.

Board had just stepped out for lunch when the call came from an editor at *Campus Life* to Sroka. "Did you get this letter about the lawsuit too? We've been in prayer all morning about it." With Steve out, she wasn't quite sure how to respond and haltingly confessed that it wasn't real, that Steve had in fact sent it. After a moment of stunned silence came the reply, "Very funny," and an abrupt dial tone. As soon as Steve returned from lunch he called *Campus Life* back to try (with only marginal success) to help his friends see the humorous side of the episode.

and put them back on the shelves, somehow thinking that they still might be useful. In order to throw them away, Wilma had to wait until Charles had gone home on trash days and then put them in the dumpster.

The Urbana conventions were also growing. While in 1961 over five thousand delegates were present, by 1970 over twelve thousand attended. So the exhibits for mission agencies and book sales had to be relocated to the University of Illinois Armory. The IVP cashiers at Urbana 70 (some were campus staff and some were volunteers) looked very official as they cranked out paper tapes from cash registers as books were sold. But this was just for an appearance of control. Nothing was ever done with the tapes, and no one ever tried to balance out a cash register. (If it came up short, what would have been done?) Only once did a volunteer cashier help himself to the contents of the till. (He was a Bible school student who presumably needed money for textbooks.)

At one point during Urbana 70 the team couldn't get the cash registers open! Ralph Gates, a campus staff member in Colorado, had worked in a grocery store and knew something about how the machines operated. So he was drafted and rescued the book team. Ralph logged many miles in his sneakers, running from one cash register to another to deliver change or make repairs.

The Schaeffer Connection

In May 1972 Jim Sire traveled to Switzerland to spend time with Os Guinness, a brilliant young associate of Francis Schaeffer's at L'Abri, to work on Guinness's book *The Dust of Death*. On his way back Jim stopped in London and met briefly with Edward England at Hodder and Stoughton. There Edward gave IVP the first option to publish the U.S. edition of *Knowing God* by British theologian J. I. Packer. Jim Nyquist commented to Sire on his return, "Your fifteen minutes in London with Edward England will probably be worth more to the Press than your ten days with Guinness." It proved to be so. While *The Dust of Death* was very successful, *Knowing God* has had an even more extraordinary publication history, eventually selling over a million copies.

Schaeffer's partnership with Sire and IVP continued to flourish. Just two months later, in July 1972, the Press brought Schaeffer to the Christian

Shown here in 1972 at the Main St. offices are (from left to right) Steve Board, Jim Nyquist and Jim Sire.

Booksellers Association convention in Cincinnati to promote *Genesis in Space and Time* and two pamphlets, *Back to Freedom and Dignity* and *The New Super-Spirituality,* all released that month. Jim helped host him.

> One evening [Schaeffer and Sire] sauntered down to the edge of the Ohio River, where barges and steamboats were gliding up and down. An off night for the [Cincinnati] Reds [baseball team] left typically raucous Riverfront Stadium looming silently over the banks of the river. As the two turned to head back toward the hotel, Schaeffer was in a characteristically dour, reflective mood. Melancholy by nature, he did not often smile or engage in lighthearted, robust laughter.
>
> During a lull in the conversation, Sire painted an intriguing scenario. He said he would have enjoyed locking Schaeffer and [C. S.] Lewis in a room and climbing up above to eavesdrop [on their conversation about topics they didn't agree on]. An unusually rich smile spread across Schaeffer's time-worn face. Envisioning the scene in his mind, he turned to Sire and said, "Oh, if we could have talked, I'm sure he would have come around."

Sire suspects the uncharacteristic smile meant Schaeffer now felt free to say privately what he had longed to say publicly! Sire did not see this as an example of Schaeffer's arrogance but of his simple confidence in his views, the power of reason and his straightforward honesty.

One L'Abri-related project that did not do well was *Portrait of a Shelter* by Sylvester Jacobs. This large-format (9" x 12") hardback book contained black-and-white photographs of those who lived, worked and studied at L'Abri (French for "The Shelter"), the name the Schaeffers gave to the study-work community they developed in the Swiss Alps. This art book was printed on high-quality paper and strikingly featured one or two portraits per page, with all but a few people identified by only their first name—or not at all. It was a beautiful book—but one that could be appreciated only by people well acquainted with L'Abri.

The plan for the book created quite a discussion at L'Abri when Sire visited there in May 1972, and many felt that such a project could commercialize L'Abri in a way that would compromise its integrity. So they decided to allow it to be published only if the connections to L'Abri were severely muted. A foreword by Francis Schaeffer was permitted, but there was no explanation anywhere in the book or on the cover that this was a book about the community the Schaeffers founded.

As a result, of course, the main reason for its potential appeal to book buyers was lost. So when 4,600 copies were printed in 1973, very few sold, and many that were ordered by bookstores didn't sell through to customers and were returned to IVP by the bookstores. As employees would sometimes wryly tell friends and visitors, "We ended up with more books in our warehouse than we actually printed." To make matters worse, as an economy measure in anticipation of strong sales, thousands of extra cloth cover boards were imprinted at the time of the first printing for use in future reprints. These of course were never used and had to be thrown away.

In May 1973, Jim Sire's own first IVP title was produced, *Program for a New Man,* a booklet that considered the writings of B. F. Skinner, Aldous Huxley and Herbert Marcuse. It did well, selling over fourteen thousand copies in its first fourteen months. Yet in another case of overexuberance and a misguided attempt to achieve a low per-unit cost, the production department (despite Sire's own considerable doubts) reprinted 25,000 copies. It took seventeen years to finally exhaust that second printing.

The Two Jims

At the time *Portrait of a Shelter* was being developed, David Alexander visited Downers Grove. David had recently left IVP-UK to start Lion, his own publishing house in England. His first major project was a seven-hundred-page, full-color handbook to the Bible. He was desperate to sell the project to an American publisher, without which the book (and probably Lion as a whole) would not be viable. Jim Sire and Jim Nyquist met with David and listened to his presentation. After he left they decided that the project just wouldn't be meaty enough to be of interest to a wide audience. Eerdmans, however, picked up the project and published it in 1973 as the *Eerdmans Handbook to the Bible*. It went on to sell over three million copies worldwide in various editions. The very people Sire thought wouldn't find it sophisticated enough endorsed the volume for Eerdmans. In hindsight, Sire saw this turn of events as one of the biggest mistakes of his tenure at IVP.

A similar project that Sire considered and pursued was that of a study Bible. There weren't as many available in the 1970s as there were twenty years later. He himself used the Harper Study Bible developed by Harold Lindsell and was familiar with the Oxford Study Bible as well; he thought these could be good models for IVP to follow. So he consulted John Stott, who he hoped might be involved in the project. Stott's reaction was clear, however. Notes ought not to be included with the Bible text since they could inadvertently be considered to be as authoritative as the Scripture itself, something he feared had occurred over the decades with the Scofield Reference Bible. So Sire dropped the idea. In retrospect, clearly it would have been a successful publishing project. But IVP would have had difficulty taking up the project in later years when a flood of study Bibles emerged from other publishers, crowding the field.

The tag team of Sire and Nyquist was back on its game, however, when they met with John White, a psychiatrist and former IFES associate general secretary for Latin America, who had moved to Winnipeg, Canada. They arranged to get together one day in 1974 at O'Hare Airport to ask White (at the suggestion of Stacey Woods) about writing a replacement for the book *Sacrifice* by Howard Guinness. This book about the lordship of Christ, originally published by the British IVP in 1936 and carried by

IVP in the U.S., was now clearly becoming dated. John agreed, and in 1976 *The Cost of Commitment* was published—his first book with IVP. As an afterthought, just as they were leaving O'Hare, Nyquist asked White to write a replacement for the old Moody Press book *The Way,* which had also been used for years as a key discipleship tool with students. John agreed to this as well, and the result was *The Fight,* which eventually sold over 300,000 copies.

John's third book published with IVP was actually his first. *Eros Defiled* had been turned down by another publisher ("because Christians only want to hear about the goodness of sex"), so he sent it to IVP. Both Jims and John agreed, however, that it would be better if the other two books were published first, so that his writings were not pegged as being of a certain sort. This proved prescient. White had an extraordinary range, from fantasy fiction to serious works on psychology. While some authors would revisit a single theme time and time again in their books, White dealt with leadership, prayer, money, church discipline, sexuality, depression, parenting, discipleship, spiritual gifts and more—all with equal skill, insight and biblical wisdom. He became one of IVP's most important authors of the seventies, eighties and into the nineties, publishing over two dozen fiction and nonfiction titles with the

---

THE FRANKFURT BOOK FAIR

In the mid-1970s Jim Sire felt it would be productive for IVP to send a representative to the Frankfurt Book Fair in Germany, the largest and oldest gathering of its kind, which regularly draws over 5,000 publishing houses as exhibitors with attendance of more than 250,000 over the five days of the event. The Fair was primarily an event where publishers sold rights for translation to other publishers. Finally he convinced Nyquist that it was worth the expense. Initially IVP joined a cooperative booth with other Christian publishers coordinated by its European agent for translation rights, Winfried Bluth. In 1981, IVP began displaying independently, but this time in cooperation with ECPA (Evangelical Christian Publishers Association). Sire kept the responsibility of representing IVP at Frankfurt into the late 1980s, after which Andy Le Peau, Jim Hoover and Ellen Hsu usually represented IVP.

Press, with a combined total of nearly two million copies in print.

White also embodied (and perhaps at times deliberately fostered) the persona of an absent-minded professor. On one occasion he told the editors that he ended up writing a particular chapter for a book a second time—because he had forgotten he had written it the first time!

The two Jims were an effective partnership, leading IVP through a period of rapid growth and change. Nyquist, the administrator/entrepreneur, and Sire, the academic/editor, each appreciated the strengths (while being aware of the weaknesses) of the other. With their two offices side by side, it was easy for one to discuss with the other whatever was needed.

Of course, Sire regularly used his considerable gifts of oral communication to persuade Nyquist to agree with him—to accept certain books for publication, certain titles for particular books or the like. Sometimes, however, Nyquist disagreed and would not be moved. At such times Sire learned to say, "Well, Jim, we're not really ready to make a final decision at this time. I just wanted to bring you up to date on where we were." Then, a couple weeks later, as Sire tells it, he would raise the issue again and, more often than not, find Nyquist to be more amenable to Sire's point of view.

Rescue from the Slush Pile

In October 1973 one important book was rescued from the slush pile (the stack of unsolicited manuscripts every publisher receives) by assistant editor Don Smith. He read a manuscript by a little-known Baptist pastor in Nebraska that was a poetic retelling of the life of Jesus—portraying him as a Troubadour. Both he and Linda Doll excitedly encouraged Jim Sire to take this imaginative manuscript seriously. In February 1974 Sire wrote the author, Calvin Miller, that IVP wanted to publish his book *The Singer.*

Months before, Miller had been waking up nights, stirred to write this tale, perhaps unconsciously inspired by the recent Broadway hits *Jesus Christ Superstar* and *Godspell.* Later Miller wrote:

> When the manuscript was done, I sent it to Jim Sire at InterVarsity Press. "It's good," he said, "but we want to think about it a couple of weeks before we give you an answer." So I waited until finally the let-

ter came. They were going to do it. Jim Sire had done his Ph.D. on John Milton, and the fact that he liked it was joy immeasurable to me. "But," he cautioned, "we're going to print five thousand of these. They may not do well—in fact we may end up with four thousand of them on skids in our basement for the next ten years. Still, it's a good book and deserves to be in print."

The distinctive interior line drawings and cover artwork Joe DeVelasco created for the original edition of *The Singer* (shown here) contributed significantly to its wide appeal.

Far more than a thousand copies sold. Actually, over three hundred times that amount sold in its first decade. It became "the most successful evangelical publication in this genre." *The Singer* was followed in two years by *The Song* (paralleling the story of the early church in Acts) and two years after that by *The Finale* (inspired by the book of Revelation). Publication of *The Singer* changed Miller's life. Even though he stayed in the pastorate for many years, it set him on a course of writing and speaking that he could not have imagined.

The books helped keep IVP in the publishing spotlight as well. When John White sent in a children's fantasy book, *The Singer* had paved the way, and so in 1978 the first of six books in what became the successful

Archives of Anthropos series was published—*The Tower of Geburah.* But neither White's editor, Andy Le Peau (who joined IVP from campus staff in 1975), nor Miller's editor, Jim Sire, gave much thought to building from here to create an entire line of fiction for the Christian market.

Others did, however. In 1979 Bethany House published *Love Comes Softly* by Janette Oke, and in 1986 Crossway Books released *This Present Darkness* by Frank Peretti. They proved that a sustained market for Christian fiction existed. Soon many other publishers were entering the market, but the editors at IVP did not see a lot of fiction that they were as strongly impressed with and so did not pursue fiction systematically. In fact, Sire

By 1976, when this photo was taken on the second floor of the Main St. offices, IVP was adding new employees rapidly.

turned down Steve Lawhead's manuscript *Dream Thief.* His elitist tendencies (he was a Milton scholar, after all) got the better of him, and he judged the book to be good but not great. Soon, as Lawhead's stock rose quickly, Sire realized his publishing error.

In the mid-seventies Francis Schaeffer's notoriety and influence were peaking. He was considered by many the most prominent living apologist for the Christian faith in an era of new intellectual upheavals in society and challenges to the church. In a cover story in *Christianity Today*, historian Michael Hamilton noted Schaeffer's influence on such diverse people as musician Larry Norman, Moral Majority founder Jerry Falwell, Bob Dole's vice-presidential running mate Jack Kemp and theologian Clark Pinnock. "Perhaps no intellectual save C. S. Lewis," wrote Hamilton, "affected the thinking of evangelicals more profoundly." IVP had a major role in Schaeffer's impact, publishing in a seven-year span fourteen different Schaeffer titles that collectively sold over two million copies.

At this time Francis Schaeffer and his son, Franky, began to formulate a major book and film project that would cover the sweeping changes that had occurred in Western thought and culture from Roman times to the present. The project was being managed by Franky, who was asking for a $100,000 advertising budget and a high rate of royalty. The year was going well financially for IVP and Nyquist knew books by Schaeffer sold well, but still it would be a significant risk. So he, with Jim Sire's agreement, decided to turn it down. (Ironically, the next year, 1976, was even stronger for IVP, and Sire realized in retrospect that financially it could have taken on the project.) Revell and Schaeffer then agreed to terms for the book, *How Should We Then Live?* But Schaeffer insisted that Jim Sire still edit the book for him, which he did for that book (and later for *Whatever Happened to the Human Race?*).

So early in 1976 Sire and Schaeffer met in Washington, D.C., to work on the manuscript during the National Religious Broadcasters Convention, where Schaeffer was speaking several times. Sire would work over the text, confer with and get some new material from Schaeffer, and then work on his own again till the next round.

Francis and his wife, Edith, had adjoining rooms in the hotel, with Jim and Francis working in one of them. Every so often Edith would burst in from the other room, excited about some bit of news from the family or friends. Each time, somewhat exasperated, Francis would say, "Edith, Edith, Edith, we are working." Each time she would finally recognize their need to not be interrupted and would leave, only to burst in again and have the cycle repeated. While the two Schaeffers bickered often, Sire knew Edith was the one who provided the steady foundation from which Francis could do his work.

FOUR VIEWS

IVP pioneered a unique format in publishing that was later copied by other publishers. The idea came from Robert Clouse, a professor of history at Indiana State University and a long-time friend of InterVarsity. He knew there was much disagreement about and intense interest in the end times among Christians—after all, Hal Lindsey's *The Late Great Planet Earth* was a mega-bestseller in the seventies. So he proposed a book that would contain four essays by four proponents of distinctly different views of the millennium, the thousand-year reign of Christ mentioned in the book of Revelation. What was even more distinctive, however, was that he proposed that each essayist write a brief response to each of the other three, and that these responses also be published in the book, following each main essay. *The Meaning of the Millennium* was a hit when it was published in 1977, and it eventually sold over 100,000 copies.

Clouse then suggested other topics be treated with a similar format, and so IVP published other four-views books he edited on war, wealth and poverty, and women in ministry (coedited with his wife). Soon others came to IVP suggesting that they edit books in this format. Four-views books were published on psychology, science, predestination and more. Other publishers, most notably Zondervan, followed this example with their own multiple-views books.

The format suited IVP well. As a nondenominational organization, InterVarsity Christian Fellowship sought to establish a wide umbrella under which many could meet. IVP lived by this same value, often choosing to address areas in which committed Christians disagreed by publishing responsible biblical scholarship on many sides of an issue rather than by ignoring the issue or choosing one position.

The four-views format also served IVP's purpose of helping broaden the thinking of Christians. Disagreement could actually contribute positively: it could make Christians think more carefully about what they believed, and it could help readers appreciate that perhaps there might be more in Scripture than was first thought.

While working with Schaeffer over a period of years, Sire was all too aware of how other scholars often critiqued Schaeffer's work in their areas of expertise. The philosophers thought he got things pretty much right except for the philosophy. The art historians thought he got things pretty much right except for the art history. And so forth. So Sire was especially vigilant when working on *How Should We Then Live?*, intended as a sweeping overview of Western culture. At one point he painstakingly worked over three paragraphs by Schaeffer on prominent nineteenth-century German philosopher Georg W. F. Hegel, basing his revisions on Frederick Copelston's landmark *A History of Philosophy*. After the book came out, a prominent evangelical philosopher told Sire that Schaeffer got Hegel wrong. Sire concluded then that such criticism was not due to Schaeffer's inadequacies but to the fact that scholars simply disagree with other scholars from time to time.

Meanwhile, the Logos Bookstore chain continued to grow, with thirty locations across the United States. While it was extremely helpful for IVP to have this inside track to information about what was going on at the retail level, it became apparent that the purposes of the chain and of IVCF were diverging and that it would be better for the chain if it gained its independence. So an agreement was reached, and in 1974 the Association of Logos Bookstores, headed by Jim Carlson, was formed as a nonprofit trade association, serving as a coordinating and support organization for all member stores. IVP kept ownership of its three Logos stores, but one by one sold them off over the next ten years to fund further publishing efforts.

One such initiative that IVP undertook with money from the sale of a bookstore was InterAction Radio. In 1978 Pam Hillery (later Proctor) was charged with coordinating a five-minute program that was aired on dozens of Christian stations five days a week. She and Diane Filakowsky (later Eble) interviewed a different author each week on a topic related to an IVP book. Later a professional announcer dubbed in the interviewers' questions. While InterAction Radio gave authors another channel for communicating their passion, it was discontinued after a few years for lack of funding and lack of evidence regarding its effect on book sales.

In the mid-seventies, a retired gentleman by the name of Clarence Ogren assisted production manager Jock Binnie part time. He had worked for years in legal publishing and so was a stickler for accuracy and precision. One of his jobs was to read through every book after it had been completely edited, typeset, double-proofed and corrected. (This was possible in a day when IVP published only twenty-five or thirty books a year, none of which were large academic or reference tomes.) No matter how carefully

TYPESETTING

In the 1960s pouring hot lead into letter-shaped forms became obsolete—the age of *cold type* had arrived. Most publishers outsourced their typesetting needs. But not IVP. On IBM typesetting machines that looked something like electronic musical keyboards, Nora Holmes, Marj Sire and (later) Gail Munroe keyed in every word of every book from typewritten manuscripts that were copyedited by the editors with blue pencils. Often messy manuscripts had been retyped to make them cleaner for the typesetters—but that meant each manuscript would be totally typed three times—when the author typed it, after it was edited and then when it was typeset.

In the 1970s IVP upgraded to a Mergenthaler system. Long rolls of yellow paper tape about one-inch wide with a sequence of holes for each character were produced by the typesetting keyboard units. These tapes were fed into the phototypesetting machine, which held "negatives" of each typeface. The photographic paper used was in long rolls inside cassettes the size of a large loaf of bread. These rolls were developed by running them through a unit containing a chemical bath, a mini-darkroom that sat on a countertop. Corrections were made on the typeset pages by the literal cut-and-paste method. The hope was that the little waxing machine stayed at the correct temperature so waxed corrections wouldn't fall off on the way to the printer. The resulting "camera-ready copy" was used by the printer to create plates for their presses.

In the 1980s the digital world came into being and IVP replaced its system with typesetting equipment from Varityper. When the editorial department adopted PCs in the mid-eighties, manuscripts were handed over on floppy disks. Now, instead of having to rekey every letter, typesetters would key in only the "tags" or codes needed to format each book. In the 1990s, desktop publishing replaced true typesetting systems, which allowed IVP to send digital output directly to printers rather than camera-ready copy.

others had worked, Clarence would inevitably find dozens of errors in each book that still needed correction. Some affectionately nicknamed him "Eagle-Eye" Ogren, only to find out later how appropriate the moniker was. He was actually blind in one eye.

Also mid-decade Herb Criley brought in IVP's first mainframe computer. (Before that time, IVP had outsourced its computing needs.) When the Micos system was installed, computer terminals started to populate the cubicles and desks of accounting and order entry. Arlie Davidson was IVP's first in-house programmer and wrote many customized programs to meet the needs of business and marketing.

As is often the case in sales and marketing departments, a series of employees funneled through in the seventies. Jock Binnie worked in sales before heading up production and typesetting. (He left IVP to join the FBI in 1980.) Dick Smiley (1975-1979) was the first IVP employee to focus on academic sales and marketing. In 1977 he initiated IVP's first academic catalog, called "The Whole Mind Catalog," which was the title used for the semi-annual publication for the next eight years. In 1978 Bob Murphy, a former campus staff member, left IVP, and Jim Nyquist looked for a replacement. He eventually persuaded another campus staff member, Ralph Gates (who had helped IVP at Urbana 70), to leave beautiful Colorado to

NYQUIST AND IFES

Jim Nyquist was energetic and always on the move. Not only did he rapidly pace the mile between his house and the IVP office twice each day, but he traveled the world when he took on responsibilities as IFES Literature Secretary in the mid-1970s, a position he held for over twenty years, more than half of that being after his retirement from IVCF. He consulted with the national sister movements of InterVarsity around the world, encouraging and advising them in their publishing efforts in many different countries. Nyquist was much beloved, appreciated and respected around the world for his efforts and his cultural sensitivity. In 1994 he published with IFES *Administry: Keeping Ministry in Administration,* a book for the boards and general secretaries of IFES movements.

He traveled light, usually taking only two well-worn leather brief cases, one with his clothes and one with his papers. He did worry from time to time that he was taking too much time out of the office with his IFES responsibilities, sometimes being gone a month or more at a time. But usually this was not a problem. He was on the go often, however, and he always sought to squeeze every minute in his schedule for all he could. Once he left the office only one hour before an international flight. On arriving at O'Hare thirty minutes later he discovered he didn't have his passport. He made a quick phone call to his family, who drove the passport to the airport, where he retrieved it from them at the curb and, remarkably, made his flight.

come to IVP to head up Bible and Life (a three-weekend training course for IV students) and to be mentored in marketing by Al Youngren.

Jim Nyquist had agreed to oversee Bible and Life because he wanted to get some of the burden off of Barbara Boyd, creator of the training program (who was stapling and shipping materials from her basement in New Jersey). Ralph stepped in to assist with scheduling, setting up leaders' training and getting materials out. Two years later Nancy Fox arrived to help Ralph, with Bible and Life as her main job. (Carolyn Boyes also joined this team and later became administrative assistant to Linda when she was director.)

HIS magazine continued its cutting-edge ways. In its February 1978 issue, HIS took a stand on homosexuality, back when most people weren't talking much about the subject. In an article titled "Was Anita Bryant Right?" HIS took issue with the former Miss America who had received national attention for leading efforts to repeal an ordinance that forbid discrimination against homosexuals in Dade County, Florida. The magazine suggested that gay people should not be denied jobs and apartments, though the article did not say their lifestyle was OK. One reader, outraged at the viewpoint that civil rights for homosexuals should be supported, tore the magazine into pieces and mailed it back: "Cancel my subscription!"

HIS also got flak for an article on the Panama Canal at the time when the United States was debating the question of returning control of the Canal to Panama. (Some folks felt that social concerns should not be addressed in a Christian student magazine, and some had a different viewpoint on the Canal issue.) Jim Conway's "A Meeting of Needs" (February 1980) was seen by some to be too soft on divorce, though today it would sound perfectly Christian and reasonable to most readers.

The Gift of Humor

Seeing humor as a gift from God, HIS also included such items as the "Jonah and the Whale Bank" (a fake ad for a fake bank—put in a dime and see Jonah pop out on the whale's tongue). A few readers, however, failed to see the humor and actually sent in orders! Another humor feature that ran in the late seventies in HIS was the "Bubble Babble" column, written by Andy Le Peau and his good friend George Carthage. Students began sending in bubble definitions of their own such as for *debatabubble*: "what a bubble puts on his hook to catch fish"; and *unthinkabubble:* "to destroy a bubble by mental telepathy."

The editorial by Linda Doll in the May 1978 issue not only honored humor among Christians but also chronicled some of the typical office atmosphere.

> I'm sitting here reading a manuscript, thinking solemn thoughts about whether it's appropriate for us in HIS magazine, when a burst of group laughter rushes in from down the hall. It brings a smile to my face and a *zing* to my whole self.
>
> They're only having a meeting down there in Jim Nyquist's office, not a party. After all, this is the Literature Division of Inter-Varsity. It's probably a discussion on the size and shape of next year's InterVarsity Press catalog, or something like that. Not rollickingly funny. But we have some exceptional humorists in this office, and every meeting is laced with lines to make Alan Alda's writers jealous.
>
> I'm surprised at myself, getting so tickled by the sound of laughter when I haven't even heard the joke. It feels good, hearing a gang of people laugh. This is life as it should be; there's something *right* about it.

Jack Stewart, who had come from campus staff to join the editorial department for two years, left to attend Regent College. He was replaced in 1978 by Jim Hoover, also a campus staff veteran. Hoover had worked for eight years with IVCF in New England. He spent his undergraduate years as a math major at Carnegie Mellon University in Pittsburgh. Subsequently, he earned a master's degree in mathematics from Stanford University and an M.Div. from Gordon-Conwell Theological Seminary.

Hoover began working three-quarters time because Jim Sire said there wasn't enough money in the budget. Beginning in the fall the workload for the editorial team was so heavy that Sire thought he would need to send some work out to freelance. Hoover said to him, "Why send it out when I'm only working four days a week?" Sire said he would have to confer with Jim Nyquist before bringing him on full time. A few days later Sire, somewhat embarrassed, told Hoover that he had made a mistake in the budget and that he could have been hired full time from the start.

Hoover's first project as an editor was to work on Richard Lovelace's *Dy-*

namics of Spiritual Life, a classic text that is still in print. Hoover had just had Lovelace as a professor at Gordon-Conwell, using a mimeographed version of the manuscript as the course text. So he knew Lovelace and his work well. Hoover especially appreciated the irony of the role reversal this provided. The student was now instructing the teacher—a reversal that Lovelace graciously and gratefully accepted.

Expanding Again

The space at the Main Street office filled up fast. The half of the upstairs that had been used for storage was swallowed up, bite by bite, for office space as more and more employees were added. Every two or three years

InterVarsity Press's 20,000 square-foot distribution center in Westmont, Illinois, nears completion in 1979.

Herb Criley brought in carpenters and electricians to build new office space. (And when he wasn't doing that, he was moving desks around. As the saying went, "If it's Friday, Herb must be rearranging furniture.")

As more storage was moved downstairs and more books were being published, books began to be warehoused offsite—and even that didn't solve all the overcrowding problems. The board of IVCF then approved the purchase of property on Plaza Drive in Westmont (just three miles away).

THE BIRTH OF *THE UNIVERSE*

Jim Sire drew his first diagram of worldviews in the early 1960s while teaching college students to distinguish Milton's theism from Hardy's naturalism and Wordsworth's quasi-pantheism. Tom Trevethan and Steve Board (both on IV campus staff in Illinios) invited Sire to give a lecture on the topic at the two-week Christian Study Project at InterVarsity's training facility, Cedar Campus, on the Upper Peninsula of Michigan. The next year Steve asked him to expand it to six lectures. Then he suggested that Sire write a book, which became *The Universe Next Door.*

Given his experience with *Papers on Literature,* Sire did not expect the book to sell well and never expected it to be adopted as a text (which it was immediately). Because he didn't expect classroom use, he intentionally avoided an academic tone and wrote it at an accessible level, which possibly is the reason it was so well received at hundreds of universities and colleges around the country.

It had enough land for a warehouse with the possibility of an office addition in the future. IVP moved its shipping and warehousing operation into the new distribution center in 1979 while 5206 Main Street was reconfigured to hold an expanding office team.

The seventies proved to be another era of explosive growth for IVP, with sales increasing about 500 percent. The bestselling books of the era that led the program included titles by Francis Schaeffer (*Genesis in Space and Time*), Walter Trobisch (*Love Yourself*), J. I. Packer (*Knowing God*), Ron Sider (*Rich Christians in an Age of Hunger*), Calvin Miller (*The Singer*), John White (*The Fight*) and Rebecca Manley Pippert (*Out of the Saltshaker*).

Jim Sire had editorial instincts that drew him to books with both high-quality content and excellent sales potential. His own book on worldviews, *The Universe Next Door,* originally published in 1976 and eventually selling over a quarter million copies in four editions, spoke of the range of topics, interests and ideas that absorbed his mind. In its publishing program, IVP was a reflection of his thought, commitments and prophetic passions. It was a very personal editorial vision, but one that resonated with the needs as well as the spirit of the times.

Sire was not one to allow fad or fancy to guide his decisions. When someone pointed out a recent bestseller from another publisher and suggested that IVP should do something similar, he responded, "Don't let someone else set your agenda." One could get in trouble trying to imitate others and doing a poor job of it. He wisely thought IVP should be true to itself, remain faithful to its call and do what it did best—of course, as he interpreted what that meant!

Stott and Packer

While new U.S. authors highlighted IVP's bestseller list in the seventies, it was a decade when IVP's British heritage bloomed as well. Mark Noll writes, "The thinking of what might be called middle-brow American

John Stott answers questions from delegates during a plenary session in Assembly Hall at an Urbana Student Missions Convention in the mid-1970s. He spoke at all four conventions that decade.

evangelicals, who are by habit and sometimes conviction systematically unecclesiastical, has been decisively influenced in the period since World War II by at least three English churchmen—C. S. Lewis and John R. W.

Stott as well as [J. I.] Packer." IVP was clearly marching a path in the seventies as the primary publishing conduit in North America for two of these three key figures, selling more copies of books by Stott and more by Packer than were sold by all other U.S. publishers combined.

In Packer's case, he "exerted that influence by combining characteristics that have rarely been joined together in America. In a word, he is an *educated, Reformed, Anglican evangelical,* with each of the four ascriptions vital as a counterweight to the other three. As the history of Christianity in America has shown so often, any of these commitments by itself can easily become a threat to clarity of Christian thought and integrity of Christian activity. Together, at least as they have been conjoined in Packer's writing and speaking, they have been water to a parched and weary land."

It was also in the seventies that Stott's influence in the United States reached new heights. In 1974 he chaired the drafting committee of The Lausanne Covenant, one of the most significant documents on evangelical doctrine and mission produced in the twentieth century. Stott spoke at all four Urbana conventions in the seventies, and his sales of IVP's edition of *Basic Christianity* (twenty years after its first release) reached all-time highs in the United States. Even twenty years later Mark Noll would write, "I consider John Stott the sanest, clearest and most solidly biblical living writer on theological topics in the English language."

Borrowing a line from Sir Isaac Newton, Jim Sire would often comment that the success of IVP in the U.S. was due, in large part, to the fact that "we stand on the shoulders of giants"—meaning the foundation IVP-US stood on was built by the books it distributed or published that had originated with IVP-UK. Clearly, the British heritage that marked IVP from its very first years was reaching its maturity in the seventies. The effect of this on the American church as a whole has yet to be fully analyzed or appreciated.

Years of Transition

The Early Eighties

InterVarsity Press

"Stick-to-it-iveness is one of the more inelegant words in the language, but I have a special fondness for it nevertheless. I heard the word a great deal when I was young, mostly, as I recall, from my mother. I was a creature of sudden but short-lived enthusiasms."

EUGENE PETERSON,
A LONG OBEDIENCE IN THE SAME DIRECTION, 1980

Decisions about which manuscripts to publish in the early 1980s were made at meetings chaired by Jim Sire and held in his office. Manuscripts would be discussed by the editors along with some representatives from sales and marketing. Six or eight people would squeeze in for what was called the "editorial meeting" (because in the sixties and seventies the editorial department made all the decisions, with Jim Nyquist's approval, since a marketing department as such did not exist). Most manuscripts came to the Press "over the transom," or unsolicited. These usually complete manuscripts were then evaluated by the team. Editors would bring reports, and discussion would ensue, but without Sire's approval the book would not go forward.

As the decade of the eighties began, Jim Nyquist felt it was time for the marketing department to increase in influence. One of the reasons IVP had been weighted toward editorial from the earliest days was that there just wasn't enough money to spend on advertising or promotion. Sales had been outsourced or handled with a few in-house employees. Some functions often handled by a marketing department were delegated to editorial because there simply was no one else around to do the work. One of Jim Sire's early responsibilities was writing the copy for the entire catalog, and that remained in editorial's hands until the late eighties. In publishing, rights and permissions were often the responsibility of sales and marketing or perhaps of the business department. Again, because IVP editorial was already involved in buying rights for books from England and had the networks in place, it also took on responsibility for selling rights to England and other countries.

With Nyquist's increasing time away traveling for IFES, he told Jim Sire that approval for publication would be given when editorial and marketing were agreed. Only if they didn't agree would he need to be brought in on the decision. Jim Sire and the other editors were not happy with this. Before, all they needed was Nyquist's approval. Now, it would seem, they needed the approval of Ralph Gates (head of marketing) as well. They felt their responsibilities were being infringed upon and that editorial integrity could potentially be compromised by sales concerns. But Nyquist was firm.

So, each editorial meeting, as each manuscript was discussed, the editors would look to Ralph for his agreement—or not. The discussions were occasionally confusing, however, because while Nyquist had been clear with Sire about the new arrangement, somehow Ralph didn't have the same understanding. He thought he was still there just to offer comment and then sell whatever books editorial decided on. Editorial was frustrated because Ralph sometimes wouldn't give a clear decision, and Ralph was frustrated because he couldn't figure out what it was that editorial wanted from him. After about a year in this befuddled state, the communication problems explicitly came out during an editorial meeting, and Ralph heard clearly for the first time from the editors that he was expected to give a plain thumbs up or thumbs down. He had had no idea this new authority

---

"OVER THE TRANSOM"

A transom is a crosspiece above a door, or between a door and a window above the door. Before air conditioning became standard in modern buildings, many offices had windows above their transoms, which could be left open for ventilation. A transom window left ajar also provided an opportunity for aspiring authors, who supposedly could get a hearing from an editor who had otherwise refused them, to toss their unsolicited manuscripts in through the opening. Thus the phrase "over the transom" came to be associated with a manuscript that a publisher didn't solicit or expect. (The "slush pile" is another common term, used to describe such unsolicited manuscripts that accumulate while awaiting review.)

It is nearly impossible today for an unsolicited manuscript to be published by a major publishing house, whether general or Christian. But smaller publishers, including InterVarsity Press, are usually still willing to give at least some attention to those that arrive over the transom. Three of the most successful "over the transom" complete manuscripts that arrived at IVP were Calvin Miller's *The Singer,* Peter Kreeft's *Between Heaven and Hell* and Eugene Peterson's *A Long Obedience in the Same Direction.*

This last book had been turned down by twenty publishers before it arrived at IVP. Jim Hoover picked it out of the slush pile and started to read. Before long he was in the hallway, grabbing whoever might pass by, and, manuscript in hand, saying, "Listen to this . . ." It was so good and so clean, he thought it was virtually ready to go straight to typesetting without any need for copyediting. As with *The Singer,* it would be the book that put its author firmly in the consciousness of the reading Christian public.

---

and responsibility had been conferred on him. Once the misunderstanding was cleared up, meetings proceeded much more smoothly.

The Urbana Fox

Nancy Fox took on responsibility for IVP at Urbana from 1981 through 1996, following Andy Le Peau who had been in charge for Urbana 76 and Urbana 79. The literature team consisted of about 120 people drawn about equally from three different groups: IVP employees, IVCF campus staff assigned to work with the book team at Urbana, and volunteers. The volunteers took a week of vacation from their normal jobs to assist at Urbana and serve the students between Christmas and New Year's. Some volunteers, such as former InterVarsity staff Denny Chadwick and his family, came to many conventions in the eighties and nineties to help with sales.

Most workers served double duty as cashiers in the Armory and as Book-of-the-Day (BOD) cashiers in the Assembly Hall, which was about a mile away. Others stocked and restocked books (led, for example, in 1987 by Doug Secker), handled accounting (with Nadine Hunt in charge), and staffed the IVP Center (handled by Joyce Nelson and Sue Bielat). And everyone helped with setup and take-down (overseen by Ed Miller in 1981 and Jeff Yourison in 1984). Jim Hagen supervised Armory sales while Jane Wells was responsible for the BOD in 1984 and Mickey Maudlin in 1987.

The BOD operation at Urbana developed to meet students where they were—coming out through the vomitoria (the doorways from the auditorium to the hallway on the perimeter) after sessions. Storing the books in the bowels of the Assembly Hall, the BOD team restocked after each morning and evening plenary session, sometimes working late into the night.

The Armory on the campus of the University of Illinois, Champaign-Urbana, housed booths for dozens of mission agencies on the infield of this indoor track. IVP's book displays and cashiers (shown here in 1979) occupied three-quarters of the perimeter of the Armory's main floor. This basic configuration was used by IVP for its bookselling operation during all the Urbana conventions of the 1970s and 1980s.

Key books were selected having to do with missions, evangelism, prayer and guidance. A single Book of the Day (usually discounted 60 to 80 percent off its retail price) might sell anywhere from 2,500 copies to 7,500 copies during the five days of the event.

THE COMPENDIUM

IVP published a compendium of the main plenary addresses given at each Urbana from 1955 to 1988. Some of the editorial folks on the book team spent their convention days holed up with the scripts of the main speakers. After the Assembly Hall was built, editors were stationed in a booth, high above the floor behind the last row of seats, comparing manuscripts of the prepared talks with what the speakers actually said. That helped them determine if the prepared text could be used in the final volume or if the talk would need to be transcribed and edited.

Joan Guest led the editorial work at Urbana 81 and Jim Hoover did so at Urbana 84 and Urbana 87. Marj Sire and Dot Bowman transcribed the tapes of addresses for which no script had been turned in. The compendium was then rushed into print by May following the convention, to fill the orders taken there.

Over the years, the compendia have chronicled the messages of key Urbana speakers such as A. W. Tozer (Urbana 54), Donald Grey Barnhouse (57), Billy Graham (57, 64, 76, 79, 81, 84), Festo Kivengere (61, 76), John Stott (64, 67, 70, 73, 76, 79), George Verwer (67), Elisabeth Elliot (73, 76, 79), Luis Palau (79), and Helen Roseveare (76, 81). Several of John Stott's best-known messages were given at Urbana, including "Jesus Christ and the Authority of the Word of God" from the 73 convention (later published as the IVP booklet *The Authority of the Bible*) and his biblical overview of God as a missionary God given at Urbana 76.

One of the most important essays recorded was Tom Skinner's talk at Urbana 70, "The U.S. Racial Crisis and World Evangelism." His soul-stirring speech that rocked the convention with its clarion call for racial justice during the heat of the Civil Rights Movement closed with the words, "The Liberator has come!" which became the inspiration for the title of the entire compendium, *Christ the Liberator.*

As the years passed, however, there was less interest in a print version of the plenary sessions, and sales steadily declined. So *Urban Mission: God's Concern for the City* edited by John Kyle, the compendium of Urbana 87, was the last one produced.

In 1987 convention director John Kyle decided on a new approach. Instead of a Book of the Day, each day he would sell packages of three or four books at just above cost. His idea was to have students take home a missions library that could last them for years. That year *Operation World* was also offered by itself for $1 each and sold 10,000 copies.

When Linda Doll, David Neff and Bud Bultmann were the HIS editors, they presented HIS at a plenary session of Urbana 81, offering a special subscription rate for the magazine to delegates. Each person had received a subscription card upon arriving. Knowing that students might not get around to it later, the editors waved around a four-foot-long "pencil" on the Urbana platform in the Assembly Hall as they showed folks exactly how to fill out their subscription blanks. Many delegates followed their instructions and were soon receiving the magazine.

Cassette tapes of plenary sessions were also sold at the Armory within twenty-four hours after each talk was delivered. That way students could "Take Urbana Home on Tape." Hundreds of others placed orders at the convention for delivery afterward. Likewise, students could order a compendium of the plenary talks, which was printed within about five months after the convention.

At Urbana 81 a secondary book sales area was set up across from the Armory in Huff Gym (now Huff Hall). There wasn't enough room for all the mission agencies and seminaries to exhibit in the Armory, so many were located in Huff. The convention organizers were concerned that traffic flow would be light at Huff, so they asked IVP to make books available for sale

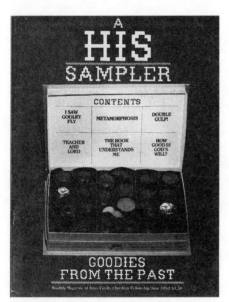

This June 1982 issue of HIS magazine featured pieces from each of the magazine's previous decades, including articles, poems and short stories by such writers as John White, Joe Bayly, Kenneth Kantzer, Luci Shaw, John Stott and Paul Little.

there too. This created an extra workload without significant increase in sales. But those team members who knew where the tunnel was that connected the two buildings could walk back and forth without fighting the weather or the traffic.

The June 1982 issue of HIS was a collection of classic pieces from previous issues and bears rereading today. HIS always tried to be both biblical and relevant, dealing with personal, campus and world issues. It published poetry by writers such as Kenneth Taylor, Luci Shaw and others. Reprint requests still come in for some of those old HIS articles and allegories, such as Harald Bredesen's "The Fish That Discovered Water" and NCF staff Sharon Fish's "Cockroaches in the Kitchen."

That was also the year of the 150th anniversary of the founding of Downers Grove, when the first annual Heritage Festival was held, drawing thousands to the middle of Main Street right in front of the office. IVP had a "free lemonade" table at the festival for several years, giving away a sample of its product: the *My Heart—Christ's Home* booklet. And Bozo the Clown performed at IVP's end of the block. Not only did IVP allow the Fest to plug in to its 5206 Main Street electricity for their stage, but Bozo was allowed to use the IVP restroom—and to make his escape out the rear fire door when his performance was over. (Seems he didn't want to fraternize with the kids on his own time.)

Director Doll

In 1983, Linda Doll was appointed director of IVP by Jim Nyquist, who was her supervisor as overall director of the literature division. The appointment evidenced InterVarsity's commitment to women as equal partners in the ministry at a time when there were virtually no women executives in Christian publishing. The immediate purpose, however, was to allow Nyquist to take on additional supervision of some of the managers in the IVCF national office in Madison, Wisconsin, with the title of administrative vice president of InterVarsity. David Neff took Linda's place as HIS editor. The IVP department heads reporting to her were: Herb Criley (business), Ralph Gates (sales/marketing), Jim Sire (editorial), Andy Le Peau (production—doing double duty in editorial with the title of managing editor), and Paul Keenon (distribution). Paul, who had been a fireman, worked on the

Linda Doll worked as a campus staff member for IVCF from 1961 to 1968, when she joined IVP. She was editor of HIS magazine from 1976 to 1983. This photo was taken during her years as director of IVP, from 1983 to 1990.

renovation of 5206 Main Street. Carolyn Boyes, Shirley Kostka and Wai-Chin Matsuoka were Linda's administrative assistants during her years as director.

Linda valued careful control of expenses. When she became director of IVP, Noel Becchetti, who had worked under Linda as assistant editor at HIS, said to others, "The party's over. Linda throws nickels around like they are manhole covers." One time Linda, legend has it, actually retrieved used plastic cutlery from the trash after an office Christmas potluck and asked people to set their used forks and spoons aside so they could be washed and reused. (The spirit of Wilma Holmes lived on, however, as employees conspired to throw the plasticware away without her noticing!)

While most people enjoyed working at IVP, there would be the occasional person who had problems.

MULTIETHNIC PUBLISHING

One of the earliest books from an evangelical publisher on the topic of racism and Christianity was *Your God Is Too White* by Columbus Salley and Ronald Behm (originally published in 1970 and reissued in 1981 under the title *What Color Is Your God?*). Its thesis that Christianity in America has historically been allied with slavery, segregation and indifference was (and still is) radical.

From that striking beginning, IVP began to grow its list of books about multiethnic issues and by nonwhite authors. In 1971 IVP published three books by Chinese American IFES staff member Ada Lum (and seven more by her over the next thirty years). Beginning in 1979, four titles were published by African American leader Bennie Goodwin (*Pray Right! Live Right!, How to Be a Growing Christian, The Effective Teacher* and *The Effective Leader*). Other key books in the eighties were Carl Ellis's *Beyond Liberation* (published in 1983 and revised as *Free at Last?* in 1996) and Thom Hopler's *A World of Difference* (1981; revised as *Reaching the World Next Door* in 1993).

As the multiethnic ministries of IVCF grew, so did the interests of IVP. Two key books for Asian Americans were published in the mid-1990s—*Losing Face and Finding*

Grace by Tom Lin and *Following Jesus Without Dishonoring Your Parents,* a team-written book by Jeanette Yep, Peter Cha, Susan Cho Van Riesen, Greg Jao and Paul Tokunaga. Manuel Ortiz, from a Hispanic American perspective, provided two titles as well—*The Hispanic Challenge* and *One New People.*

IVP began sponsoring a series of writers' consultations to encourage the development of books from specific groups. In April 1998 twenty men and women arrived at IVP's office for the African American Writers' Consultation (hailed by participants as the first of its kind anywhere), which was chaired by IVCF area director Tony Warner and IVP editor Rodney Clapp. The three days of discussions covered the process of publishing and particular proposals writers brought. In January 2000 a similar gathering for Asian Americans was chaired by staff author Paul Tokunaga and IVP editor Cindy Bunch. A third was held for evangelical women in the academy in April 2002, with leadership from Mary Stewart Van Leeuwen and IVP editor Dan Reid.

IVP continued to expand its range of titles with books like *King Came Preaching* by Mervyn Warren (2001) and *On the Jericho Road* by J. Alfred Smith (2004). Its bestselling title in this arena was *More Than Equals* by Spencer Perkins and Chris Rice (1993; revised 2000), selling over 40,000 copies.

Since 1970, IVP has published over one hundred titles on topics of multiethnic interest or by nonwhite authors (see appendix 3). With well over 60 percent of these still in print, IVP plans to continue to expand its offerings since, as the demographics of America continue to make dramatic shifts, these issues will be of growing importance to the shape and effectiveness of the church.

Once a package arrived in the mail (possibly from a disgruntled former employee), and inside was a tray of lovely homemade fudge. A note said something like, "Our InterVarsity chapter appreciates the work you folks do, so here is a little gift." Turns out the fudge was heavily laced with a chocolate-flavored laxative. The folks who were most hungry that day paid the highest price.

The editorial department grew around Sire as an extension of his personal gifts and unique publishing vision. His growing stature as an author and lecturer gave IVP a visibility that aided in attracting quality authors. Sire acted, largely, as the department's only acquisitions editor, the only editor who would initiate contact with or solicit new works from authors. He delegated most of the development of manuscripts to others. In his early years, he was not overly concerned with the potential commercial viability of manuscripts, and in the period of roaring growth in the seventies, that didn't matter too much. Most titles sold well, and some sold very well. His instincts were mainly on target. His priorities were the publishing worthiness of each piece, the quality of its ideas and the unique interest each book held for him. The highest compliments he could (and did) give to manuscripts were, "The author clearly agrees with me on this," or "That's how I would have put it."

At times his personal interest overcame (or made irrelevant) his publishing instincts. One such case was *The Wind Is Howling* (1977), a spiritual autobiography of Ayako Miura, a Japanese novelist. Sire, a Ph.D. in English, convinced himself that Miura was more well-known than she actually was. Even in the roaring seventies the book sold very poorly. Likewise, Sire's appreciation of the British commentator Malcolm Muggeridge persuaded him to publish *The Practical Christianity of Malcolm Muggeridge* by David Porter (1984). Sire's appreciation did not extend to the Christian reading public. Sire's own book *Václav Havel*, published in 2001, continued his streak of intense interest in—and IVP's apparent willingness to continue to publish—books about quality writers who were underappreciated by book buyers.

His interest in the new religious movements, however, lined up very well with the needs of the campus and the church. Many booklets such as *The Moon Doctrine* (1976) and books such as his own *Scripture Twisting* (1980) sold tens of thousands.

Sire's instincts for quality were always sharp. Why else take a chance on a twenty-three-year-old, newly minted graduate of Wheaton College and publish him on such a sophisticated topic as existentialism? But that is how *Despair: A Moment or a Way of Life?* (1971) became the first book written by C. Stephen Evans, who went on to a noted career in philosophy.

Sire also embraced the core campus values of evangelism, discipleship and missions, and many books on those topics were published. But he cared little for Bible study guides, and so, even though he wrote one himself, the Press published few during his tenure. On the other hand, the intersections of culture and Christianity held his full attention. Marxism, Buddhism, politics, economics, sociology, literature, philosophy—all these and more captured his notice, especially as they took up issues of the day.

His voluble personality also dominated discussions. During one editorial meeting, when a new member of the marketing team showed signs of impatience at the way Sire ran such meetings, taking many opportunities to talk on tangents only loosely related to the business at hand, Al Youngren tried to calm things down by explaining with a wry smile, "You've just got to get used to the rhythm of editorial—five minutes of work means five minutes of fun."

The Fourth of July weekend in 1983 started a bit earlier than planned at InterVarsity Press. An article in the IVCF newsletter to staff headed "Tree Bites Building" reported:

> Friday morning, July 1, a severe storm swept through Downers Grove, IL, causing a tree to blow against the InterVarsity Press building. [Marj Sire, Gail Munroe, and Melody Bourland were inside— Marj was terrified to see the tree coming directly toward the building, not swaying but coming straight at her.] The tree took a bite out of the northwest corner of the roof and crushed power lines against the window over the typesetting office. We lost power in the whole building and had to close the office at 10:15 am. Office manager Herb Criley worked swiftly to arrange for the tree to be removed and the brickwork repaired. And now, it's back to business as usual.

Another crisis occurred when some birds built their nest in the window air conditioner for the typesetting room. The equipment in the room required a climate-controlled environment, so Herb Criley said the nest had to go. Soft-hearted Gail and Marj practically signed adoption papers, and when Herb removed the nest they "threatened" violence. A "Typos" song titled "Herbie and the Birdies" memorialized the calamity at Herb's going-away party a few years later.

Brave New Publisher

In the spring of 1984 IVP published a book from IVP-UK called *Brave New People* by D. Gareth Jones, a bioethicist teaching in New Zealand. The book looked at the ethical issues facing society at the beginning of life that technology had just begun to push into public consciousness—in vitro fertilization, genetic screening, cloning, artificial insemination and abortion.

Almost immediately an uproar ensued. The Christian Action Council published a strongly negative review in their newsletter, *Action Line,* and urged their readers to write InterVarsity Press. The book thoughtfully weighed the pros and cons of abortion in the most extreme cases, such as when a baby is born without a brain. Though the author stated that cases such as these were the only situations in which abortion might even be contemplated (and never recommended), the whole book was condemned.

HERBIE AND THE BIRDIES

Marj Sire and Gail Munroe wrote the following and sang it to the tune of "Blue Danube" at Herb Criley's farewell party in 1984.

Outside our wall (tweet tweet, tweet tweet)
We heard them call (tweet tweet, tweet tweet)
Our sparrows so dear (tweet tweet, tweet tweet)
Who brought us great cheer (tweet tweet, tweet tweet)
The Fifth of July (tweet tweet, tweet tweet)
We bid them good-bye (tweet tweet, tweet tweet)
We thought they had grown, and had flown
Far from good old IVP.
Then we got the word of the fate of the birds—
Good old Herbie killed the birdies!
Air conditioning they were threatening.
So he gave the word, "Those birdies have to go!"
The typesetters sad
Thought that Herbie was bad
Until then the day arrived
When found that our birdie friends were still alive!
O joy! O rapture pure!
Oh, our birdies are secure!
Yes, their families have increased—
Termination didn't faze them in the least.
We'll miss you, good old Herb
Every time we see a bird.
Hope your new job's a success.
Now our birdies won't have to worry about their nests.

Within a month of the review, IVP received over two hundred letters and phone calls. Within five months letters from over four hundred people were received. Almost nine out of ten were from people who had not read the book. IVP had never experienced such an uproar. Jim Sire drafted a standard letter of reply and worked feverishly to make a case for the book inside and outside the Fellowship. He made phone calls to the author in New Zealand, once miscalculating the vast time change and waking Jones up in the early morning hours. He solicited and received endorsements for the book from leading evangelical thinkers such as Carl Henry, Kenneth Kantzer, Vernon Grounds, Arthur Holmes and many others. He also developed a flyer that IVP used in defending the book.

Leaflets against the book were distributed at the CBA convention in Anaheim that July in an effort spearheaded by Franky Schaeffer, whose father, Francis Schaeffer, had died on May 15, 1984, not two months before. Calling for a boycott of all IVP books, Franky labeled *Brave New People* "pro-'therapeutic' abortion." Joe Bayly commented, "Franky is in the midst of grief over his father's death. We must make allowances for his intemperate language and not prematurely judge him a loose cannon."

Bayly further quoted Franky as saying, "InterVarsity Press once printed the books of my father, Dr. Francis A. Schaeffer. I am glad that he did not live to see this recent travesty, this amalgan [sic] of dishonesty, published by a company largely built on the money made from his books." Bayly commented, "Franky might more accurately have said that his father's writing career was built on the superb editorial work on his earliest manuscripts by Inter-Varsity Press's James Sire, the Maxwell Perkins of contemporary Christian publishing. . . . And as the first director of Inter-Varsity Press back in the 1950s, I have more of a vested interest in its doctrinal integrity than the Schaeffers."

The IVP office in Downers Grove was picketed by the Christian Action Council on August 7. A few IVCF donors threatened to stop their support to field staff if the book was not withdrawn. In an attempt to allow cooler heads to prevail, on August 16 IVP sent mailgrams to all IVCF managers and asked for their assessment of the situation and their counsel. IVP management presented the results that there was minimal loss of donations and made a case that the book should remain in print. Ultimately, however, on

Brave New People, **originally published in**
England by IVP-UK, was also released in 1984
by IVP in the United States.

August 29, IVCF president James McLeish announced the decision that the book would be withdrawn from publication. In a letter sent to those who wrote protesting its publication, he said, "I am recalling the publication because the book has caused confusion which was not the intention of Inter-Varsity or the author of the book." As Linda announced the decision to the department heads and plans were made to take an excellent book out of circulation, it felt to her as if she was presiding over a funeral.

It was a traumatic event that marked IVP for many years. Thereafter, nervous editors hovered over every word in a book that said anything about abortion. It also marred IVP's editorial credibility with prospective authors who were sometimes reluctant to place their book with IVP, wondering if it too might be withdrawn from publication if the political heat brought to bear from one direction or another ever became strong enough.

Of course, those opposed to Brave New People hailed the decision, and it certainly had the effect of ending their criticisms. But several Christian leaders offered more cautionary evaluations of the success of the campaign against the book. The chair of the materials science and engineering department at Stanford, Richard Bube, wrote: "By buckling under to political pressure, Inter-Varsity has jeopardized its own integrity for all the Christian students and faculty who look to it for guidance and support in troubled times."

Richard Lovelace, professor of church history at Gordon-Conwell Theological Seminary and author of *Dynamics of Spiritual Life,* wrote, "The Schaeffers have disfigured their testimony against abortion by the slander and false witness against Christians in their most recent books. Franky is right to urge us to start using the boycott. But what can we think when he uses this weapon to force an evangelical publisher to withdraw a book which opposes abortion with arguments he considers defective? Rome at the height of the Inquisition only put books on the Index—never publishers or bookstores."

Another author, Steve Lawhead, also with a book in IVP's list, wrote of Franky's call for a boycott of all IVP books:

> Such are the tactics of those who fear the free contest of ideas so much that they have to fix the match. . . . InterVarsity Press bowed to all the pressure and withdrew the book in question. In retrospect, maybe they acted too quickly. Maybe their decision was based more on potential loss of support than on a concern for the marketplace of ideas. Maybe. One thing is certain. InterVarsity was outmaneuvered by narrow-minded invective and left waiting for evangelical support that never came.

Historian Mark Noll's evaluation was this: "In 1984, when InterVarsity Press published a book by an antiabortion New Zealander who nonetheless questioned the all-or-nothing mentality of some pro-life positions, a well-orchestrated campaign of demagoguery forced the publisher to withdraw the book."

In the aftermath, Eerdmans made an immediate decision to publish the book, in a slightly revised form, in 1985, receiving some protests but no major effort to have the book withdrawn. This proved what one picketer of IVP at the CBA convention said when "asked why they chose IVP when several other Christian publishers had published books even more strongly pro-abortion. 'We couldn't shape up the others.' In other words, they felt that they could effect change at IVP through the leverage of the nationwide student movement to which it is related." And so it was.

Five months later, shortly after Gordon MacDonald replaced James McLeish as president of IVCF, Linda Doll asked the new president if he would write her a letter of support that she could show to prospective authors to allay any lingering concerns they might have. He did so, saying, "We must do our best to publish responsible books and at the same time resist the pressures of any single-issue group which would attempt to inhibit the spirit of publishing freedom."

In October 1985 MacDonald also wrote to the author, D. Gareth Jones:

I have read your article in the ASA Journal [about your experience with the protests against *Brave New People*] and am even more appreciative of what the past year or two have brought you in the way of pain and struggle. I'm sorry. Although I had no part in the decision surrounding the withdrawal of BNP from the IVP list, I feel extremely bad and embarrassed about it all. It is a low point for all of us in IV/USA.

It was hoped that MacDonald's efforts to show the regret of the Fellowship as whole would be a significant step in bringing healing to the author. It certainly did to InterVarsity Press.

Leadership Turmoil Again

Across the nation, one of the bestselling books of 1984 was a novel that had actually been published thirty-six years before—George Orwell's *1984*. This dystopia, a dark look at the future and its infamous Big Brother, had become synonymous with authorities who controlled all aspects of life, directing not only what people would do, see and read but even what they would think. The irony, of course, did not go unnoticed by those at IVP who had experienced the effects of a well-run emotional campaign to ban a book.

As 1984 moved forward, the tumult continued as the publishing house was swept up in another stir that was embroiling the national movement of InterVarsity. Jim McLeish, who had been appointed president of IVCF following the retirement of John Alexander in 1981, was pushing many changes forward. Some in IVCF found these to be invigorating while others across the movement felt they were disruptive.

Serious morale problems existed among some staff leaders in the field. . . . The conflict orientation of McLeish's leadership became a burden to some of the regional directors. With an accountant's background, Jim McLeish tended to quantify the task, making expansion a premier value. The staff felt the rift between [the national office in] Madison and the field widen.

One of the initiatives that affected IVP the most was McLeish's plan to centralize all marketing in the movement into the hands of the development department at headquarters in Madison, Wisconsin. IVP made the case that promoting a nonprofit organization dependent on contributions and selling books in the competitive marketplace were very different enterprises. In addition, there would be no economy of scale or expertise gained. For IVP books to be marketed from outside IVP—right along with the marketing of Urbana, camps, staff members who needed support from donors—would not be an improvement for IVP or the rest of the movement. But McLeish was not persuaded.

The leadership at IVP was still reeling under the decision regarding *Brave New People.* Now these other proposed shifts seemed likewise to indicate a lack of understanding about how a publishing company operated. As a result Herb Criley, IVP's business/office manager for eighteen years, decided to take a job with David C. Cook Publishing Co. in Elgin, Illinois (now Cook Communications Ministries in Colorado Springs). Ralph Gates also felt that these changes were deeply philosophical in nature and not just administrative. So he also decided it was time to leave, and he likewise went to Cook. Curtis Arnold, who had come in from the field staff to do the campus liaison job, became sales/marketing director, and Jim Hagen was hired to replace Herb Criley.

For months Jim Nyquist and Peter Northrup, senior vice president for IVCF, had listened to the complaints of campus and office staff. In the fall, Nyquist and Northrup went to speak to McLeish together about the problems, asking if the three of them could approach Board Chair Allen Mathis. "Later both put their thoughts in writing. [But] McLeish was unresponsive to their concerns."

On Jim Hagen's first day at IVP replacing Herb Criley, November 5, it was announced that Peter Northrup had resigned a few days earlier, giving no public reason for his departure and leaving Jim Nyquist as the only vice president in the Fellowship. Hagen wondered what state of turmoil he had walked into. His uncertainty was increased as discussions ensued about the possibility of combining the national office and IVP, possibly in Madison, Dallas or Atlanta. Having just moved from Nashville and having just purchased a home in Downers Grove, Hagen did not look forward to such a prospect. Neither did most at IVP or at the national office in Madison.

Jim Nyquist felt he must do something to alert the board that the philosophical issues and ministry implications were very serious. Many at IVP spent a great deal of time in prayer with Nyquist and with each other. He asked their counsel, and many discussions ensued. He worked on several letters but hesitated to send any. Finally, "since the president had ignored his several requests for a meeting with the board chairman and the president during the preceding months, at the end of Urbana [84] Nyquist distributed a letter describing his evaluation of the situation to all board members." This violated a recent directive that staff were not to make direct contact with the board. They could only communicate through the supervisory structure. The letter was not received well. The board felt it heard nothing from Nyquist that it didn't already know. Many thought that sending the letter was an act of insubordination and that, given Nyquist's views, it would have been more appropriate for him to have simply resigned as Northrup had.

After the stressful and dispiriting staff conference that followed Urbana 84 and three more difficult weeks, the board of IVCF met January 25 and 26, 1985, and decided that Jim McLeish and Jim Nyquist would both be retired immediately. Gordon MacDonald was appointed president by the board, and Ron Nicholas (who had been a campus regional director and then head of the development department for IVCF) was soon afterward made Linda Doll's supervisor.

While there was resolution, there was not immediate relief. IVP employees had universal respect and appreciation for Nyquist. Many felt he had been the messenger who had been shot for delivering bad news. It was very difficult to see him leave under such circumstances, and the Press felt battered, shaken and uncertain about the future.

Jim Nyquist, nonetheless, left a clear legacy to IVP and a solid foundation on which to build. Under his watch IVP grew twenty-one times in sales. The core values and ethos of the wider Fellowship became even more firmly embedded in the publishing program—commitment to the lordship of Christ, being university-minded, a worldwide perspective on the work of the church and more.

He placed a premium on finding strong, qualified people and then setting them free to do the work. He also augmented IVP's fiscal conservatism with a willingness to take calculated risks for the sake of ministry. He encouraged the development of the Press-O-Matic book club, The Rack, InterAction Radio, InterVarsity Records, Logos Bookstores and more. Not all proved to be long-term successes, but that fact created an atmosphere where there was freedom to fail. In addition, many of these initiatives continued to serve InterVarsity and the wider church for decades. Growth for the sake of growth was never his goal. Expanding the reach of Christ's kingdom was always foremost.

In the years that followed, Nyquist continued to serve as IFES Literature Secretary helping national movements around the world with publishing and administration. During those years, he and McLeish were also able to reconcile, repairing their relationship and putting behind them the issues that had once separated them.

Something that helped put many others at ease was Gordon MacDonald's early decision as president not to move either IVP or the national office. Without this distraction, people could more easily center on the ministry of InterVarsity.

Years of Regrouping

The Late Eighties

INTERVARSITY PRESS

"I could never myself believe in God, if it were not for the cross. The only God I believe in is the One Nietzsche ridiculed as 'God on the cross'. In the real world of pain, how could one worship a God who was immune to it?"

JOHN STOTT, THE CROSS OF CHRIST, 1986

Jim Sire had been on sabbatical during the last half of 1984 (spending part of that time teaching at New College—Berkeley). He told Linda Doll that he didn't want to come back to the same job description, and they decided that he would work half time for IVP, with the title Senior Editor, and half time on campus as a lecturer in the areas of worldview, apologetics and evangelism (something he had been doing increasingly in recent years). Andy Le Peau then started supervising the editorial department, maintaining the title of managing editor, with Nancy Fox appointed by Linda to take Andy's role as production manager. (Over the years Sire increased his percentage of time with the campus until his retirement.)

Le Peau's first connection with IVP had been a copy of the British edition of *Escape from Reason* a friend had given him during high school. He then

SIRE'S INFLUENCE

Jim Sire's travels after 1984 took him in the next decade and a half to universities across North America and around the world. Roger Olson, author of many books on historical theology, including several from IVP, evaluated Sire's contribution to evangelicalism through his books and speaking this way:

James Sire of IVCF and IVP has influenced a large number of evangelical students and others through his lectures and books. [He] and other IVCF speakers and writers have in common a broad evangelical appeal that is clearly postfundamentalist in mood while vigorously promoting a conservative version of Protestant philosophy and theology. Especially Schaeffer and Sire have delmonstrated Christianity's power to critique culture both prophetically and philosophically while strictly avoiding blanket condemnations of culture and urging readers and hearers to engage with secular and pagan culture.

Jim Sire had been traveling increasingly to lecture at college campuses around the country in the early 1980s. At mid-decade he decided to begin doing that half time, while still working for IVP half time. In the following years his work on campus steadily increased, including many trips to universities around the world, especially Eastern Europe.

became part of the InterVarsity chapter at the University of Denver. It was during that time that he first met Don Smith at Bear Trap Ranch, InterVarsity's training facility in the Colorado Rockies. Don, the assistant editor at IVP, had come to Bear Trap to do Bible and Life training. As the two sat together at a meal, Andy asked what Don did. As Don described it, Andy's first thought was, *That's exactly what I want to do.* Later, after coming on InterVarsity campus staff, Andy met Don again in 1974, this time at IVP in Downers Grove during New Staff Orientation. He visited Don's office and asked him again to show and tell him what he did. Andy's reaction was the same as the first time. When Don left IVP six months later to take a job at David C.

Cook, Andy applied for the opening and was hired.

Ten years later Andy was a task-oriented manager who strode purpose-fully up and down the hallways seeking to maximize every minute of the day. His people skills were not quite as seasoned, however. Linda regularly exhorted him to take time with the other editors, talk with them, let them know what he was thinking. Following in Sire's footsteps was no small task, but Andy put himself into it energetically.

Jim Sire traveled to dozens of campuses around the country and was eventually traveling regularly to Eastern Europe to lecture on topics related to *The Universe Next Door*, which was soon translated into Croatian, Bul-garian, Czech, Polish, Romanian, Russian and Serbian, as well as other Eu-ropean and Asian languages. But whenever he was in town he would gather whoever was interested in joining him for lunch down Main Street, Downers Grove, at his favorite spot—The Brass Bagel. Sometimes it was only an audience of one or two, but that was all he needed to speak expan-sively about whatever topic of the day struck him. Reference Book Editor Dan Reid recalls that Sire would even on occasion bring along a chapter of a book he was working on and read it to those assembled.

Inductive and small group Bible study had been a hallmark of InterVar-sity campus work since the 1940s. Several staff wrote study guides for IVP, but other former staff and those influenced by them began to popularize this method. For example, former staff Marilyn Kunz (who had trained at The Biblical Seminary of New York, as had Jane Hollingsworth) and Cathe-rine Schell started a not-for-profit ministry in 1960 called Neighborhood Bible Studies to publish their guides. Harold Shaw Publishers produced Fisherman Bible Studyguides by Maggie Fromer, Gladys Hunt, Sharrel Keyes, Carolyn Nystrom, Luci Shaw and others who were also trained in the inductive method.

Andy Le Peau drafted a proposal in 1981 for IVP to reclaim its heritage in the field of Bible study (*Discovering the Gospel of Mark* and *Look at Life with the Apostle Peter* being two of IVP's first homegrown publications with several other Bible study guides being published over the years). The time seemed right for a fresh emphasis in this area. So the decision was made in 1982 to hire campus staff member Jack Kuhatschek, a grad-uate of Dallas Theological Seminary and Regent College, to lead the charge. As it turned out, Jack had asked Jim Nyquist a few years before why IVP didn't publish more Bible study guides. Obviously, the job fit Jack's interests and background.

Together Jack, Andy and Jim Hoover conceptualized what became Life-Builder Bible Studies (soon after renamed LifeGuides). The first seven guides were introduced in 1985, and they almost immediately became the top-selling series in the industry. (By 2004 over 10 million LifeGuides were in print.)

Jack was also responsible for designing the publishing world's first shelf display for Bible study guides. He knew that without spines, Bible studies could easily get lost on bookstore shelves. Every time he went into a bookstore, he would rearrange the LifeGuides, which were inevitably in a messy pile.

So Jack talked to art director Kathy Burrows about designing something like a cardboard "shelf talker" (a sign on the shelf that would call attention to LifeGuides). But Kathy knew how quickly cardboard displays began to show

Jack Kuhatschek and Kathy Burrows collaborated to create the industry's first Bible study guide shelf rack, which was copied by many others.

wear, and how quick store owners were to toss them after a few months. She thought they should create something more permanent that could be used for years, as The Rack was. She envisioned something like a wire shelf rack. The conversation took only about sixty seconds, but it was pivotal.

Jack took Kathy's wire rack idea and converted it to acrylic, sketching a rough drawing on the white board during an editorial meeting. The holder would fit on a shelf and allow the guides to be displayed face out to maximize use of space. He even went further to construct some cardboard mockups. Production Assistant Shirley Peska refined the final idea and got bids from manufacturers. The LifeGuide shelf display became very suc-

PROOFREADING

Before the days of digital technology, edited manuscripts would need to be completely rekeyed during typesetting. To ensure that the book was copied correctly and completely, IVP usually had page proofs "double proofed." That is, one proofreader would read the original manuscript aloud to a second proofreader who would read the typeset version, making corrections as they went along. Not only were the words read aloud, but so were punctuation, capitalization and indentations. "Stop" meant a period, "exclam" indicated an exclamation point, "com" was used for a comma, and so forth. Anyone of a certain vintage who was listening might be reminded of Victor Borge's comedy routine about punctuation.

Shirley Wheaton worked as a proofreader at IVP for eighteen years, the first ten of which were before the digital era. Being in the habit of reading punctuation aloud did create an embarrassing moment for her in church once, however, when it came time for the responsive reading. Once when everyone else paused at the end of a sentence, from habit she blurted out, "Stop!"

cessful, and most other Christian publishers of study guides copied it.

Jack Kuhatschek also pioneered the editorial department's use of personal computers in editing in the mid-eighties. Those who were used to blue-penciling manuscripts were skeptical. Were IVP authors using this new technology anyway? Would they really send in manuscripts on floppy disks? Andy and Jack decided to send out a survey to authors to find out if they were using PCs and if so what kind and what kind of software. When the results came back, the department was amazed. Over two-thirds of IVP's current authors were already using PCs. Obviously IVP was behind the times, and so the Press went digital.

Soon a PC was installed for each editor—containing two floppy drives and no hard drive! In order to run a program, it was installed in one floppy drive and the document saved on the other floppy drive. With no network, to print out a manuscript editors would walk down the hall, floppy disk in hand, to the one PC that had a printer connected to it.

Healing the Wounded, a new book by John White and Ken Blue, was released at the 1985 CBA convention. IVP made buttons for the booth reps that said, "Have you read White and Blue?" It was corny, but not as bad as some of the CBA items. (A favorite was a comb and mirror set that had stamped on it, "With God all things are possible.")

That was also the year IVP published *Sandy* by Leighton Ford, the moving story of Leighton's oldest son, a passionate Christian involved with InterVarsity in college, who died of heart problems at age twenty-one. It became a *Campus Life* Book of the Year and IVP's first major trade hardback bestseller. IVP began publishing more trade books in cloth after this, though paperbacks still predominated.

Marketing Director Curtis Arnold saw that the decor of Christian stores was changing and that the old black wire rack that had given IVP such vis-

The original wire rack (left) served IVP for over fifteen years and gave IVP substantial brand recognition in Christian bookstores. The round rack (center), adopted in 1987, was forced into early retirement because of mechanical problems and replaced by a square, rotating edition (right).

ibility in the marketplace was rapidly going out of style. So in 1987 he developed a large, round, white plastic rack which affectionately (or derisively) became known as "The Water Heater." Mechanical problems (it didn't turn easily) forced IVP at great expense to replace it just three years later with a different model. While this relieved many problems, ground was lost in The Rack program from which IVP would never entirely recover. Compounding this problem was the trend in bookstores to move away from publishers' displays so that they could sport a unified interior design in the store.

Reference and Popular

In the early 1980s IVP trade book sales (which was most everything IVP published) had plateaued. IVP was facing competition from those who likewise sought to produce serious-minded books. Multnomah's Critical Concern series, launched in the early eighties, was making a mark. So were books of cultural analysis from a new publisher, Crossway Books, which began in 1979 as the book-publishing division of Good News Publishers, which was known as a tract publisher. Soon, under the leadership of Lane and Jan Dennis, Crossway was publishing books by Francis Schaeffer, Martyn Lloyd-Jones, John MacArthur, J. I. Packer, Chuck Colson and John Piper. While Crossway's books would often take a viewpoint of Christianity standing against culture rather than engaging culture as was the case for IVP, there was still some overlap, not only of authors but of perspective.

Was there a solution? Over the decades, IVP had taken several reference books from IVP-UK, such as the Tyndale Old Testament Commentaries, the Bible Speaks Today series and large academic books such as *New Testament Introduction* and *New Testament Theology* by Donald Guthrie. The latter book had had a significant financial impact on IVP when it was released in March 1981. When sales in March 1982 took a huge downturn comparatively, it took a while for Andy Le Peau and Ralph Gates to figure out that Guthrie's book had been the reason the previous March had been so strong. And the fact that such books sold steadily year after year showed how stabilizing reference books could be to the company's finances. So Linda approved Andy's recommendation that IVP move forward with a reference list of its own rather than remain dependent on England. To do this,

IVP needed a full-time reference editor to take on such massive efforts. Seed money for the editor's initial salary came from the sale of one of the Logos bookstores IVP owned.

In January 1986, Andy hired Dan Reid (who had a Ph.D. in biblical studies from Fuller Theological Seminary and had taught at a seminary in the Philippines) to develop a line of reference books. He immediately began work on IVP-US's first homegrown reference book—the *Dictionary of Christianity in America* (which was ultimately published in 1990 and was named in 1991 the *Christianity Today* Book of the Year).

Discussions by those in editorial and marketing also emphasized the possibility of developing a more "popular" line of books (that is, books more accessible to a wider range of readers) to meet increasing competition from other Christian publishers and to further diversify IVP's publishing program. The idea was that IVP would continue to produce substantive books for which it was best known, such as those by John Stott, J. I. Packer, Eugene Peterson, John White, Howard Snyder and others. At the same time it would develop other books for general lay readers in the tradition of *Out of the Saltshaker* by Rebecca Manley Pippert and *Sandy* by Leighton Ford. With popular author Gordon MacDonald now president of IVCF, there were also hopes that some of his new titles could be added to IVP's list.

Le Peau felt it could be best to get some editorial help from outside IVP, to bring in some external expertise to expand this type of publishing. So while completing his search for a reference editor, in 1986 he began looking for a popular books editor. This resulted in the hiring of Don Stephenson—who had worked as a pastor and in both the editorial and marketing departments of Word Publishing in Waco, Texas.

One of Stephenson's first tasks was to pick up a project initiated by Joan Guest. Joan had come to IVP in 1977, working in the customer service department, and later was invited by Jim Sire to join the editorial staff. Joan left IVP shortly before Don's arrival in June of 1987, pursuing other publishing interests and an MSW at Aurora University.

In the fall of 1986, Joan had made an appointment to have lunch with a pastor in the area who was gaining prominence for his rapidly growing ministry. Joan had become interested in initiating projects rather than merely working with what came over the transom. With Sire not directing acquisitions as closely as he had before, there was more room for other editors to expand into this arena. She thought it would be a good idea to visit Bill Hybels, who in 1975 had founded Willow Creek Community Church in nearby Barrington, Illinois.

Hybels told her he was very focused on his church and didn't really want to be distracted with writing books. But he did agree to send IVP audio tapes of a series on prayer that he had recently preached. After Don arrived, he listened to all the tapes, worked up a proposed table of contents, and sent that along with a contract to Hybels in November 1987. He then arranged for writer and editor LaVonne Neff (who had worked at IVP from 1981-1983) to transform the tapes into a manuscript. Never one to let grass grow under her feet, LaVonne finished the draft less than two months later, in January 1988. The text was then revised and approved by the author.

What to title the book was a challenge. With so many books on prayer, how could it stand out and be appealing? As the team brainstormed, Jack Kuhatschek thought of the quote from Martin Luther: "I have so much to do [today] that I should spend the first three hours in prayer." So Jack went to the board and wrote "Too Busy to Pray" and then put "Not" above it. *Too Busy Not to Pray* thus became the final title. The book was published in August and became Bill Hybels's bestselling book, with over 600,000 copies now in print.

A Creative Culture

Deciding to develop new emphases in Bible study, reference and popular books was not entirely a top-down affair. During the middle eighties, meeting after meeting took place, including the key stakeholders in editorial, marketing, finance and production.

IVP had inherited a collaborative culture from the campus movement, which was founded quite deliberately as a *Fellowship* and not as a corporation or business. IVCF chapters were to be student-led. Staff were expected to equip students to do the ministry rather than use a hierarchical model of leadership. In addition, InterVarsity was affected by its own mission field—the university, with its traditionally generous spirit in pursuing truth while encouraging sound reasoning and fair persuasion. This collegial character and collaborative culture was not as extreme, however, at

IVP as it was in the rest of the IVCF—after all, there was a business to run, and it wasn't prudent to spend extended periods of deliberation before decisions were made.

At the same time, the culture was not as corporate or hierarchical as in many other Christian publishing houses. Many at IVP, especially in the editorial department, instinctively felt it was part of their work to participate in the wider, more strategic decisions that were made. With the two strong, longtime leaders of Nyquist and Sire less in the picture, this tendency increased markedly in the last half of the decade, in marketing and other departments, especially as these new initiatives were afoot.

HIS magazine changed its name to *U* magazine in 1986, but its monetary woes and limited subscription base continued. The leadership in Madison consulted with Linda Doll and Verne Becker about the brutal financial facts (for which there seemed to be no solution) and then made the reluctant decision to stop publication in 1988—its forty-eighth year.

It was replaced by *Student Leadership Journal* or *SLJ*. Robert Kachur moved from assistant editor at HIS to be editor of *SLJ* in Madison, Wisconsin, at the national service center of IVCF. Bob Fryling, national director of campus ministries there, was interested in helping the magazine serve campus interests more directly and so encouraged the move. After Robert left for graduate school, Jeff Yourison (former campus staff and former campus liaison at IVP) became the editor. This magazine was tailored for InterVarsity student leaders rather than Christians in college more generally. Copies were sent free of charge to InterVarsity staff who put them in the hands of their students. While there was no income from subscriptions, this was offset substantially because the expensive process of subscriptions/renewal notices/bookkeeping/address changes had been eliminated. (The fall 2005 issue was the last printed issue as Jeff Yourison and the *SLJ* editorial team launched studentsoul.org the next year—a web project aimed at broadening InterVarsity's resource offerings to a larger audience.)

The IVP Christmas Party continued to be a highlight of each December. Usually it was held in a local church basement such as at Gloria Dei Lutheran, First Methodist or First Presbyterian, all in Downers Grove. A grownup's version of a talent show followed dinner with specially written songs and skits highlighting the quirks of publishing and office life. In the seventies Jim Nyquist annually brought down the house with his Swedish-accented rendition of " 'Twas the Night Before Christmas." One year the theme was inspired by the popular public radio show *A Prairie Home Companion*. The Garrison Keillor-like monologue rendered by Jack Kuhatschek focused on Jim Sire and hilariously exaggerated the way he filled his day sharpening pencils, getting a cup of coffee in the lunchroom and chatting, or taking a walk in the snow, and never quite getting anything done. These endearing quirks and foibles were balanced by Jack's more serious reflections on Sire's attitudes toward work, friendship and the Christ of Christmas.

Computer Conversion

One of Jim Hagen's early decisions had been to hire Ron Lanier on July 15, 1985, to replace Steve Palmer as head of data processing. Hagen was on vacation at a campground when the offer with Ron was finalized by phone. The two of them soon decided that after more than ten years of service, the Micos system should be retired. This raised many questions with the national office. Lanier and Hagen spent one or two days a month in Madison

INTERNATIONAL RIGHTS AND TRANSLATIONS

IVP was not the only organization born in 1947. So was the International Fellowship of Evangelical Students (an umbrella organization of independent national collegiate movements around the globe, which included IVCF-USA). IVP's affiliation with IFES gave IVP immediate international recognition. Various IFES movements had distributed the English-language IVP books to their staff and students just as IVCF-USA had once distributed IVP-UK books in the United States. So it was natural that these movements would be interested in translating some of these titles as well. The Bible study guide by Margaret Erb, *Basic Christianity,* became one of the first, contracted for translation into Chinese in 1964 by Campus Evangelical Fellowship of Taiwan. A handful of others followed.

In 1971, Winfried Bluth visited Jim Sire in Downers Grove. Bluth had grown up in Germany during World War II, had worked with Scripture Union in England for fifteen years and now was starting a business as an agent for Christian publishers in England and America, seeking to place translation rights in Germany. He worked nonexclusively for IVP for two years before signing an exclusive contract for the German language on April 1, 1973. Soon other northern European languages were added and a steady stream of contracts began to be written through Bluth's connections.

When Andy Le Peau arrived in the mid-seventies, translation contracts were added to his responsibilities. Later Jim Hoover took his turn as well with assistance from others. Rhonda Skinner helped international rights take a significant leap forward when she attended a meeting with rights managers from other publishers and caught a vision for proactively selling rights. When Rhonda's husband Kevin (who also worked at IVP) took a job in another state, Ellen Hsu took on rights duties, including meeting with international publishers at the CBA convention and at the Frankfurt Book Fair. IVP worked most frequently with the IFES-linked publishing houses in thirty-three countries, but spread far beyond that as well.

Through the decades over twelve million copies of IVP books have been sold in translations into over 63 languages including Korean, Chinese, Portuguese, Spanish, Croatian, Urdu, Thai and Russian. IVP has contracted translations with over 400 publishers in over 50 countries.

Some of IVP's most widely translated books include:

- *The Fight* by John White (30 languages)
- *The Universe Next Door* by James W. Sire (21 languages)
- *Too Busy Not to Pray* by Bill Hybels (20 languages)
- *Daring to Draw Near* by John White (17 languages)
- *The Mark of the Christian* by Francis A. Schaeffer (15 languages)
- *My Heart—Christ's Home* by Robert Boyd Munger (15 languages)
- *Tyranny of the Urgent* by Charles E. Hummel (14 languages)
- *Excellence in Leadership* by John White (13 languages)

discussing whether IVP could fill orders for Twentyonehundred Productions (aka "2100"—IVCF's multimedia division) products and whether Madison could handle all payment and income processing for IVP. Eventually, it became clear that the operations of a publisher in the competitive marketplace and a work that depended on charitable contributions were just too different to create any significant efficiencies in this way.

Hagen and Lanier then pursued a publishing software package that would best suit IVP. On June 30, 1987, they cut over to a system from Computing Information Services (CIS), just in time for the new fiscal year beginning

July 1. It was a warm Tuesday night, and with the windows open, Hagen and Lanier enjoyed the Downers Grove Park District summer concert from Fishel Park right behind the office as they made the conversion a reality.

As is often the case with such turnovers, some sales and accounting history was not converted, and it took a few years to work back in the customized features that had been slowly built into the Micos system. Overall, however, the conversion went smoothly. Accounting, order entry, inventory, sales analysis and royalties were all included. Later Ron Lanier added systems for production scheduling and Urbana book sales management as well as a host of other customized features.

Railroad to the Nineties

As 1989 began, Mickey Maudlin announced he would be leaving IVP's editorial department to work at *Christianity Today* (*CT*) in nearby Carol Stream. He had been at IVP for almost six years, working his way up from an entry-level position to general books editor. But an opportunity arose for Mickey when Rodney Clapp left a vacancy at the magazine. Rodney had

IVP—INTERVARSITY PARTIES!

Parties and celebrations of various kinds have been a long tradition at IVP. Office Christmas parties in the 1970s were held at Jim and Ruth Nyquist's house on Dunham Road in Downers Grove. When it became too squeezed for the forty-some employees and their spouses, it was moved to a restaurant or church basement.

In the late seventies, several women decided to start sharing a Christmas luncheon of homemade fare. The aromas wafting out of the typesetting room, where they set up their event, were too much for the rest of the office, and eventually everyone was invited to participate. So at noon, about a week before Christmas each year, tables were spread, folks brought homemade specialties and most ate more than they should have. Often group caroling would open or close the event. The tradition still continues.

In the early 1980s, Paul Keenon, who replaced Wilma Holmes as the head of the distribution center, suggested having a company summer picnic. So another annual gathering was added to the calendar.

Employees and their families were invited to Hummer Park in Downers Grove for volleyball, square dancing and activities for the children. One year Nancy Fox organized an elaborate softball game, complete with T-shirts for the two teams (the John White Sox and the Paul Little Leaguers), cheerleaders, a play-by-play announcer and scoreboard. But the game got a bit more competitive than expected. So it was fortunate that the hotly contested match ended in an 11-11 tie.

In the 1990s other activities began to be programmed, such as visits to a minor league baseball game of the Kane County Cougars or to an outdoor Shakespeare theater. These were alternated with the traditional picnic, which moved to Ty Warner Park near the Westmont facility.

Farewell and retirement parties would often become quite elaborate as well. Skits and songs became traditions for retiring or departing long-term employees. "The Typos"—an ad hoc group organized by typesetters Gail Munroe and Marj Sire—were often called on to set their own words to familiar tunes. Marj Sire actually broke tradition by writing her own skit for her retirement in 1996. Kathy Burrows also broke tradition by catering her own farewell luncheon in 2002 as a thank you to everyone. Nonetheless, the skit commemorating her years at IVP had plenty of riotous material to work with, given Kathy's uniquely blunt and artistic personality.

The business and accounting department began its own tradition in the nineties with a Valentine's Day Open House. They provided a variety of sweets and savories appropriate for the occasion so folks could come by, enjoy and chat a bit during the day.

Community is a critical component of what has made IVP tick. Employees found spiritual nurture and friendship in the office that was rare in other settings. When Sue Bielat died in early 1996 due to illness, only a few weeks after her last day at IVP, the office held a memorial service because the family did not want a funeral. Jim Nyquist would tell employees that IVP wasn't a church and that they shouldn't act as if it were their church. Yet for many employees IVP was more of a Christian community for them than anything else.

wanted to work part time and go to school part time for a couple years in order to finish his master's degree, but *CT* felt his position needed to be full time. So Rodney left *CT*.

When Andy began looking for someone to replace Mickey, Don Stephenson suggested he contact Rodney, who was going to school and filling in with freelance work. Andy and Rodney agreed on a plan whereby he would work part time while school was in session and full time otherwise for the next couple years. After that, Rodney would become permanently full time. So Rodney and Mickey ended up taking each other's jobs.

In the gap between Mickey and Rodney, Mickey's responsibility for humor books was passed on to Cindy Bunch. Earlier Mickey had helped Cindy learn the editorial ropes. In the spirit of Tom Sawyer, who got his friends to whitewash the fence by acting as if it was great fun, Mickey decided he would magnanimously offer to Cindy, who was still relatively new, an opportunity to do some "real" editorial work. He told her that he saw her potential and thought she might be able to evaluate manuscripts that came in unsolicited. Eventually she realized that being responsible for the slush pile was not necessarily a great honor. In any case, the mentoring paid off as Cindy was able to take on IVP's Bible study line when Jack Kuhatschek moved to Zondervan in early 1990.

About this time a tradition in the editorial department began when Kathy Carlson (sister of Distribution Center Manager Paul Keenon) started putting in a few hours of administrative work each week for Dan Reid in addition to her work in the distribution center. Rhonda Skinner decided it would be good for the rest of the department to get to know Kathy and so invited Kathy and the team to the lunchroom at 3 p.m. one Wednesday for some microwave popcorn. The department met again the next Wednesday, and a custom became established that continues to this day.

Creativity showed itself in marketing as well. The legendary Georgia train trip took place during the July 1989 CBA convention in Atlanta. Allen Knight had replaced Curtis Arnold in 1987 when Curtis took a marketing job back in his home state of Kansas. Allen, a great lover of trains, arranged for IVP to sponsor a scenic train ride to Stone Mountain in order to promote the popular books developed by Don Stephenson for the general trade—Saltshaker Books. The cost would only be about as much as a full-page ad in *Christianity Today.*

Knight invited bookstore owners and buyers to come free. Authors of Saltshaker Books strolled through the cars of the train, chatted with folks and signed books. Individual box suppers from Chick-Fil-A (a regional favorite) were to be provided for everyone on board. But the Chick-Fil-A people didn't believe the number of people IVP intended to feed, and they didn't provide nearly enough boxes. So Knight arranged to get more later—but the last cars never got supper till almost ten o'clock! So, besides

---

WHY HUMOR BOOKS?

IVP's line of cartoon books was published between 1988 and 1996. Some wondered why a publisher whose tagline at the time was "For Those Who Take Their Christianity Seriously" would produce such books. But Jim Hoover often commented, "We even take our humor seriously." And so it was not unexpected that IVP would have a theology of humor. Rob Portlock says in the introduction to his *Way Off the Church Wall,* "God gives us reason for joy in the midst of life's hard times. I hope this book will add to that for you."

And in his foreword for *It Came from Beneath the Pew,* Calvin Miller says:

Rob Suggs's gift of humor to those who sometimes forget that laughter is medicine strong enough to cancel fatigue, cleanse boredom and lighten the heaviness we thought might crush us. . . . He is not a cartoonist for the squeamish or those who have declared with acid churchmanship, "Christianity is no laughing matter." The truth is, his cartoons remind us that the church always contains, within its thousands of relationships, places where laughing is a sound response. . . . So let us gather in joy, laughing not at the sacred, but the faults and foibles of our own frailties. Our laughter will not make us stronger, but it will channel God's grace into human understanding. And we will bless the laughter by which he wraps his grace in joy! And, as one of the martyrs reminds us, joy is the most infallible proof of the presence of God.

---

the fact that supper was late, that the air conditioning on the train was unable to cope with the Georgia heat and humidity, and that the trip took about two hours longer than planned, everything went perfectly! Most people were actually very gracious about it.

Over the decade the increase in IVP sales slowed down compared to previous decades, but still they nearly doubled. Every time IVP's annual sales hit another million-dollar benchmark, the office celebrated with a cake. The eighties had been a decade of some turmoil and transition. A book had been forcibly withdrawn from publication for the only time in IVP's history. Long-time director Jim Nyquist had left under difficult circumstances. Jim Sire had changed roles. Sales had struggled. Nonetheless, new ventures in popular books, Bible study and reference gave new energy and new prospects for the years to follow.

Moving and Moving Ahead

The Early Nineties

I V P

"Stripped of all the theological debates and boiled down to
its raw essence, Christianity and Christians will be judged by
two actions: how much we love God and how well we demon-
strate that by loving our neighbor. This is Christianity in a
nutshell. But pushing these two great commands to the back
pages of our practical theology has allowed Christians to join
in with the world in separating along racial lines."

SPENCER PERKINS AND CHRIS RICE, MORE THAN EQUALS, 1993

The 1990s began on a note that carried over from the previous decade.
On January 25, 1990, IVP leadership announced that four full-time and
four part-time employees were to be let go. IVP had been hovering just
above red ink for a couple years. The years of turmoil in IVP and the
broader organization had taken their toll along with recessions in the
eighties and a flattening of the Christian book market generally.

The significant expenditures associated with Saltshaker Books without
commensurate sales didn't help either. While the books sold reasonably
well (five to twenty thousand copies each), unwarranted enthusiasm over

initial sales led to excessive reprints, which meant that eventually as many books were remaindered (sold off at less than print cost) as were sold at regular price. In addition, in an effort to make the new line a success, extra money was spent in trade and consumer advertising, but this proved ineffective.

Barney Ford, who now supervised Linda Doll and IVP from Madison, was emphasizing the need for IVP to show a surplus every year. All of these pressures converged on Linda and the department heads, convincing them of the need to act. Their consensus was that payroll costs had become too high, having grown (from 26 percent to 30 percent of sales over the previous decade) without a commensurate growth in sales.

IVP's office services department was eliminated, which meant, among other things, that photocopying and office mail delivery would now be handled within each department. A job each was also eliminated in credit, order entry and production. In a workplace that had a family feel, this was an agonizing decision for the leadership team, and the office was deeply saddened by it as well.

Morale took a dive, and the leadership determined that IVP should operate in a way that would never make such a move necessary again. While taking calculated risks would be necessary in the future as they had been in the past, the department heads saw an obligation not only to fulfill IVP's mission in new and more effective ways, but to do so in a manner that would honor the employees by not putting their jobs unnecessarily at risk.

Even before those difficult days arrived, Linda Doll had been feeling that she was more skilled at editorial work than financial spreadsheets and long-range planning. So on her own initiative she announced in June 1989 that she would step down as director. After an extensive search, Ken DeRuiter was hired in March 1990 with the title Executive Director. Ken had retired from the U. S. Navy with the rank of Commodore and had owned a chain of four Christian bookstores in New Jersey. Linda then took on the role of associate editor and reported to Andy. She was happier than she had been in years.

Ken was beloved by the employees at IVP for his friendly demeanor and winsome smile. He made a habit of walking around the hallways, greeting folks with his resonant baritone voice, chatting briefly about their lives and their work, making each person feel special. One unique practice that he occasionally engaged in was especially endearing to the team. On an afternoon in late fall, he would replace receptionist Audrey Ward's familiar voice on the intercom, and begin a long ramble on what a rare, warm and sunny day it was, perhaps the last like it for many months—and then suggest the whole office take the rest of the day off. What was not to love?

During his days in the U.S. Navy, Ken had learned Russian, and it came in very handy when he made forays to the Moscow Book Fair with other Christian publishers as part of the work of ECPA (the Evangelical Christian Publishers Association). One year in the early nineties, just as the Soviet Union was reforming into several new nations, he had trouble getting his visa on time. He left the United States without it, expecting it to be faxed to passport control at the airport in Moscow. But when he arrived, the visa had not. So he spent quite a bit of time talking in the office of a Russian colonel who was to decide if Ken would be denied entry and sent back to America. The colonel was very impressed with Ken's Russian and asked where he learned it. Thinking diplomatically, Ken answered, "In New Jersey."

After a good bit of discussion, the officer finally said, "I don't know why I'm doing this, but I'm going to let you into the country."

Ken had won him over, as he did so many.

A Day in the Life of a Book

It takes a village to publish a book. In the nineties it was no different. While editorial acted as the research and development department of IVP, the rest of the organization completed the publishing process. Once books were typeset and proofed, Nancy Fox's production department went into gear. Don Frye, the dapper (though prematurely balding) production coordinator for books, was responsible to work with printers, getting the best print price he could with the quality and schedule desired for each project. He also was responsible for ordering reprints of books, which could happen two or three hundred times a year. He and Nancy took pride in being out of stock less than virtually any other Christian publisher—as attested by bookstores and distributors alike.

Getting printed books into the hands of customers and readers was the job of the sales and marketing department. Don Stephenson did double

CONNECTIONS TO THE INDUSTRY

In the early days IVP had an ambivalent relationship to the wider evangelical publishing industry, just as it was ambivalent about American evangelicalism generally. IVP participated in CBA from the earliest days since this was obviously important for sales. But when the Evangelical Christian Publishers Association was formed in 1974, Jim Nyquist was not sure the expense of membership was worth it, though he eventually was persuaded to give it a try. Despite the helpful information and cooperative efforts, the semi-annual meeting for publishers and the heads of marketing at ritzy resorts was just not IVP's style.

But as the industry matured and IVP grew, more connections were naturally made and became more necessary. Andy Le Peau was frustrated that while ECPA offered meetings focused on marketing and finance, there was no venue specifically for Christian editors from across the industry to gather and learn from each other and outside professionals. So in 1990 he approached colleagues in the Chicago area at Crossway Books, Harold Shaw Publishers, Moody Press, Tyndale House and Scripture Press about hosting such a gathering.

The result was the 1991 Midwest Christian Book Editors Conference, held on April 25-26 at the Hilton in Lisle, Illinois. Over fifty attended the event with Vic Oliver of Oliver Nelson Books offering the keynote. Mark Fackler of Wheaton College, Jerry Jenkins of Moody, Don Stephenson of IVP, Steve Board of Harold Shaw and others offered workshops. The event continued over the next dozen years, dropping "Midwest" from the title and growing to over 120 in attendance.

The Editors Conference became the inspiration for similar ECPA events for rights managers and marketers. It eventually moved, being hosted in 1999 and 2000 by publishers in Grand Rapids, in 2001 and 2002 by those in Nashville, and finally in 2003 in Colorado Springs before being folded into ECPA's Publishing University in 2004 along with its other training events.

It was in the mid-nineties that IVP also had its first ECPA board member. Ken DeRuiter served one three-year term. Bob Fryling later joined the ECPA board, where he became influential on several matters, serving as its secretary from 2004 to 2006. Whether or not IVP was still ambivalent about the evangelical publishing world, it was certainly more connected.

duty as an acquisitions editor in editorial and as director of sales and marketing, replacing Allen Knight in the latter role in 1990. Don was a tall Texan with a booming voice and a large personality (suited to his home state) that filled any room he entered. Unlike many in publishing who specialized in one aspect of the work, he enjoyed both halves immensely. He worked long hours, often arriving well before others and staying after most had left. His energy was sustained by a case of Diet Dr Pepper, which he kept at hand in his office at all times. Likewise his 64-ounce Big Gulps from 7-Eleven were constant companions. Bringing considerable marketing savvy from his days at Word Publishing, Don would soon significantly boost IVP's efforts.

Another friendly Texan in marketing during the early nineties was Bob Allums, who visited key accounts, including bookstore chains and distributors, as IVP's national sales manager. Greg Metzger also fit the mold of being a big-boned, buoyant member of the department. He had been a member of the InterVarsity chapter at Illinois Wesleyan University and took on the job of sales and marketing to campus ministries, especially to IVCF staff, of course. Nancy Iglesias, as marketing manager, enjoyed the department as much as anyone, with her ready smile and outgoing personality. She was constantly finding creative ways to promote IVP's line at CBA. T-shirts, buttons, water bottles—whatever she could come up with to draw attention to the booth. She had the perfect touch for hosting authors and managing their book signings at the convention as well.

The department did have its quieter side, however. Sally Sampson continued in her role as copywriter and project coordinator that Allen Knight had originally hired her for in 1988. Also an InterVarsity alum from the chapter at Illinois Wesleyan, Sally put her writing and organizational skills to good use with the multitude of marketing pieces—catalogs, order forms, brochures, flyers and more. She teamed up with Shirley Peska in production to get all of these printed and, when necessary, mailed out.

Deborah Keiser wore several hats as manager of marketing operations and international sales. Her dry wit balanced off the department well. She supervised order-entry team leader Marj Jaffke (who had come to IVP in 1977) and the rest of her team, including Sue Bielat in customer service and a half dozen others. (Through the late eighties, order entry had been under Jim Hagen's business department because of its significant reliance on and interaction with the computer mainframe.)

Once Stephenson's team generated the sales, the orders went to the distribution center (DC) in Westmont for shipping. Kathy Rich would pick up the orders at Main Street on her way to work three miles away at the DC in the early morning hours each day. (It was so early that sometimes the Downers Grove police tried to ticket her when they saw her car outside the office, thinking she had parked there all night.) Doug Secker was already experienced at supervising the DC, having done the job since 1986 when he replaced Paul Keenon.

Doug's dry wit also emerged from time to time. When Don Stephenson was helping with the physical inventory at the end of June one year, he was bent over counting some cartons and stood up a little too quickly, knocking his head with a resounding boom on the steel racking just above him that was holding pallets of books. Don nearly rendered himself unconscious. Flatly, Doug commented, "You only do that once."

Doug's quiet efficiency kept orders moving out the door in good order. Even so, he and his team of eight were challenged when Don Stephenson decided IVP needed to offer same-day turnaround to stay even with the competition. If orders came in by 10 a.m., they would go out the door that day. It was a difficult adjustment reworking the systems, but it came to pass.

The business department intersected closely with the rest of the office—after all, authors and printers had to be paid (not to mention employees!) and bills needed to be sent and money received from customers. Jim Hagen hired Jim Luedtke in 1991 to relieve some of Hagen's burden by supervising the accounting department. That team has rivaled the editorial department in stability with five members who as of this writing each have over twenty years of service with IVP—Nadine Hunt, Nancy Bucklin, Julie Isenberger, Florita Lopez and Judy Hessel.

Jim Hagen, known around the office as "Mr. Graph" for his quarterly office-meeting presentations of company finances, continued to oversee a group of employees each with their own unique talents. Ron Lanier provided continual maintenance and upgrading of CIS in data processing. The editorial department was certain that no one could replace Dot Bowman's remarkable speed and accuracy in word processing when she retired (for the first time) in 1991, but Hagen found her equal in Gloria Duncan. Arnold Young, possessor of the consummate servant spirit, was always ready to go the extra mile to get a package out on time or find catalogs in storage in his role in general services.

The public voice of IVP, however, was receptionist Audrey Ward. Authors, bookstore owners, printers—everyone seemed to know Audrey by name and always enjoyed hearing her warm alto voice. When leaving the office, every employee knew they would hear from her, "Have a good one!" And she always meant it.

At Urbana Again . . . and Again

Every three years or so IVP would once again put significant effort into the Urbana Student Missions Convention. Why would a publishing house do that? There was a practical reason in the early years—IVP sold a lot of books, about a month's worth of sales in just five days. But even when Urbana sales started becoming proportionally smaller, IVP was still there in force. Why? There were a number of other reasons.

Often IVP would publish several books on missions, urban ministry or evangelism, primarily to be released and sold at Urbana. It was also an important opportunity for IVP employees to have face-to-face contact with the students and staff who were a part of the larger ministry. And Urbana, of course, shared IVP's values and ethos with a commitment to bring the kingdom to the world with a holistic brand of discipleship.

In addition to her duties as production and fulfillment manager, Nancy Fox continued to oversee IVP's Urbana sales operation. About two-thirds of the office staff continued to join Nancy at Urbana—sometimes doing a job related to their regular work, and sometimes engaging in something totally different, like cashiering. (Those who stayed behind were mostly those in the order-entry department and the distribution center, so books could continue to ship to regular customers.)

Jim Hoover led the Book-of-the-Day team during five conventions from Urbana 90 to Urbana 03. In 1993 he was assisted by Greg Jao and Sue Bielat. At Urbana 93 the "package concept" ballooned to include four books and a video. IVP was uncertain of the sales potential and so Urbana director, Dan Harrison, agreed to take financial responsibility while IVP provided sales services for the program.

The packages also created huge logistical problems, only one of which was finding room to store the dozens of pallets devoted just to BOD sales in the Assembly Hall (and offsite) and to distribute these around the perimeter of the building. The sales results were also poor because the packages were bulky (students had only so much room to pack) and the video proved undesirable to them. About five thousand packages for each day were brought to the convention but thousands of packages went unsold. After that experience, IVP once again took on the financial risks of the program while sharing responsibility with the convention director for decisions about what titles were selected, what quantities were ordered and what the selling prices would be. So when Urbana 96 rolled around, IVP once again began selling only one Book of the Day at a time. But now a different book was sold in the morning and in the evening rather than the same book morning and evening as was the case before.

Don Frye acted as Nancy's "Number Two" in 1993, and Al Hsu did so at Urbana 96. Doug Secker continued to watch over stocking shelves at Urbana during the nineties. Nancy Iglesias and Deborah Keiser (Urbana 93), and Tricia Koning and Bobbi Jo Heyboer (Urbana 96) were responsible for the IVP Center (the communications center of all IVP operations at Urbana).

A major change for IVP came at Urbana 90 because the Armory had been remodeled, reducing the amount of floor space for IVP and mission agency exhibits. A new floor plan was proposed that would give IVP and 2100 about a third of the floor space in a rectangular shape rather than having the book exhibits circle the perimeter of the floor. The plan proved to work extremely well. It brought all IVP personnel closer together, made communication easier, and made it possible to stock books with inventory in just one place on the floor rather than trying to have three identical book sales areas as before.

Don Stephenson headed up a team of folks who worked furiously to put together and stock a dozen different packages of two or three IVP books on topics like evangelism, relationships, missions and so forth—all sold at a substantial discount. Jim Luedtke and Nancy Bucklin took their posts along with others in the "Eagle's Nest"—the code name for a room on the

fourth floor of the Armory, with a police guard, where all the money counting was done, away from the crowds. Somehow calling it "The Money
Room" just didn't seem to be the best for security.

Andy Le Peau headed up a team who worked in three book information
booths that were spread around the bookselling area in the Armory, each
headed with a large sign that read, "Got a Question About Books?" The
team was responsible to answer thousands of questions from students. The
most common ones had to do with the location of restrooms, but many
students asked for book recommendations. Sometimes they knew what
book they wanted and just needed to be pointed to the right shelf.

A memorable interchange occurred at an information booth during Urbana 96 when Greg Jao was approached by a female student eager to find
Elisabeth Elliot's book *Passion and Purity*. The book had sold out, so Greg
told her that and suggested another book or two that might be just as helpful. But she insisted that he find her *Passion and Purity*. When Greg ex-
plained that there simply was no copy of *Passion and Purity* left anywhere
in the building, she swore and stalked away, full of passion but apparently
in need of some purity.

Going Academic

After a variety of informal conversations over a period of months, in March
1991 Andy Le Peau, Dan Reid, Jim Hoover and Rodney Clapp met and
concluded the time was right to map out a strategy for developing more
academic books to add to the Bible study and reference lines. IVP had
arisen out of a campus ministry with an ethos that took the university seriously, on its own terms. Even so, several key facts had coalesced. First,
there were few evangelical publishers seeking to fill the academic niche.
Second, IVP had an editorial team that was well suited for such work. And
third, there was a large potential pool of qualified authors.

Many of these potential authors had been inspired as students by the
books of Francis Schaeffer in the seventies (many of them published by
IVP), which communicated that intellectual pursuits by Christians were a
valid, viable and important enterprise to undertake. "Schaeffer was instrumental in popularizing and legitimizing the life of the mind for many
twentieth-century evangelicals." Thus IVP could now benefit from the ef-

fects that IVP books had had on a generation of readers who had seriously engaged the academic world, pursued higher education, received Ph.D.s, taken positions at universities and seminaries, and were now ready to start writing significant works. Here was one indication of what Jim Sire wrote in his introduction to the thirtieth anniversary edition of *The God Who Is There*: "It is little exaggeration to say that if Schaeffer had not lived, historians of the future looking back on these decades would have to invent him in order to explain what happened."

The plan was to increase from about three to six academic books a year and to begin looking for a dozen primary texts, including an Old Testament theology, a systematic theology and an ethics text to be published over the next several years. (The program grew even faster than projected. In mid-decade IVP released seventeen academic books one year, and five years after that it released thirty-two in a year.) In addition to supplemental and survey texts, plans also called for the editors to acquire seminal or groundbreaking works "in which scholars can explore vital interests, respond most profoundly to the challenges of the day, exercise creativity to its full extent and make a contribution to knowledge. These are also the books through which IVP might most powerfully fulfill a stated purpose of the Press: to speak the gospel in the context of the university."

In the fall of 1991 the *Academic Alert* was also birthed—a substance-oriented newsletter to professors that would not look like a marketing piece but would include interesting interviews with authors and articles offering a behind-the-scenes look at significant new academic books from IVP. The interviews with authors, offering information not found in the books themselves, worked extremely well, with comments from the *Alert* even being quoted in other scholarly publications. Greg Metzger began to expand his duties from campus ministries to other academic marketing as the list grew. Bobbi Jo Heyboer, who joined marketing in publicity in 1994, soon caught the vision as well and became one of the champions for the academic program.

Helping to get things rolling, Rodney Clapp contacted Donald Bloesch about his systematic theology—and in short order the first volume of his major seven-volume work, *A Theology of Word and Spirit,* was published in 1992. Grant Osborne's contract with Thomas Nelson was cancelled when

Nelson decided to close down their academic program, and so IVP was able to pick up his new major text, *The Hermeneutical Spiral*, which was released the same year. IVP's academic line was off and running.

Three Conversations

Three other publications early in the decade spawned major conversations in the culture and in the evangelical world. The first had its origins in the mid-eighties when Jim Sire met David Cole, chairman of the biochemistry department at the University of California—Berkeley, through Jim's longtime friend and writer Walt Hearn. David thought a certain law professor at Berkeley might be interested in giving to Jim's financial support for the campus ministry part of his job. So Sire made contact, and the law professor started sending Sire pieces of a manuscript he was working on concerning defects in the logic of the theory of evolution. Sire expressed interest in the possibility of IVP reviewing the manuscript for publication and sent the professor his comments.

By the time Sire had a long walk with the professor on July 5, 1990, in Tilden Park in Berkeley, he had already agreed to publish it with Regnery Publishing in Washington, D.C. Sire then raised the possibility of IVP copublishing it with Regnery since the market channels of the two publishers were largely distinct. The author contacted Regnery with the idea, and Andy Le Peau followed up with Regnery from the other end. An agreement was reached, and in May 1991 both houses published in hardback *Darwin on Trial* by Phillip Johnson. Both editions sold well, and two years later IVP negotiated with Regnery for the exclusive trade paperback edition.

It was the beginning of a revolution. Not only was this 200,000-copy seller the first of six books IVP would publish with Johnson (the other five solely with IVP), but Johnson became the father of a movement that soon took on the name "intelligent design" (ID). One key scientist he influenced was Michael Behe, professor of biochemistry at Lehigh University in Pennsylvania, who saw a "dismissive" review of *Darwin on Trial* in *Science* magazine and wrote a letter to the editor, criticizing the review. Johnson then got in touch with Behe, introduced him to other critics of Darwin, and helped Behe find an editor for his book *Darwin's Black Box*, which became one of the most potent opening salvos in favor of intelligent design.

In ID was the nascent hypothesis that would seek to unseat evolution as the only scientific explanation for the origins of life. But Johnson's ambitions were grander yet. He sought to fracture the entire naturalistic worldview that undergirded not only science but also law, education and the entire public square.

Soon IVP published more in this vein such as *The Creation Hypothesis* edited by J. P. Moreland (1994) and *Intelligent Design* (1999) by William Dembski. By the end of the decade the movement was thriving. With every criticism and condemnation that came their way, Johnson uttered his delighted response, "What a victory!" Why? They were making such an impact that the establishment had to take them seriously. Intelligent design was on the public radar and hit a peak in August 2005 when President George Bush sparked a national discussion, telling Texas newspaper reporters in a group interview at the White House, "Both sides ought to be properly taught . . . so people can understand what the debate is about."

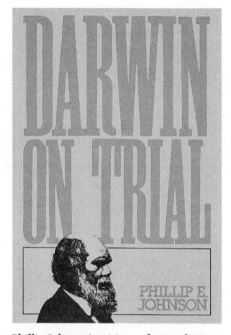

Phillip Johnson's critique of naturalistic evolution in *Darwin on Trial* became the seedbed for the intelligent design movement, for which he became the father figure.

InterVarsity Press launched a second major academic conversation among evangelicals with the publication in 1994 of *The Openness of God,* a collection of essays by Clark Pinnock, John Sanders and others that proposed a way of viewing God and his work called "open theism." Eight years earlier, in his chapter in IVP's four-views book *Predestination and Free Will,* Pinnock had first suggested that "God limits himself in relation to free human persons, such that even God does not know with absolute certainty what they will do with their free will until it is determined." Roger Olson notes that "Pinnock's 1986 essay caused some surprise and consternation among conservative evangelicals. . . . Real controversy, however, broke out after the 1994 publication of *The Openness of God.*" In this book, acquired by Rodney Clapp, the authors contend that traditional understandings of Scripture are wrong to ascribe impassibility to God (being unaffected by earthly circumstances, particularly suffering) or to claim that God knows the future in complete detail. The book makes a historical, philosophical, theological and biblical case to this effect.

Other IVP "openness" books followed, such as Gregory Boyd's *God at War,* as well as books criticizing "open theism" such as *No Place for Sovereignty* by R. K. McGregor Wright. Books on both sides soon emerged from

CONTROVERSIAL BOOKS

InterVarsity Press never sought to publish controversial books for the sake of controversy. The editors over the decades have felt IVP's calling was to allow God's Word to speak to the church and society unimpeded by cultural expectations or tradition-bound interpretations. Sometimes this meant it came in a corrective or even prophetic vein.

Your God Is Too White, published in 1970 at the height of racial unrest and uncertainty in the nation, was a radical statement from an evangelical perspective. Likewise Ron Sider's 1977 book *Rich Christians in an Age of Hunger* upset many with his challenge that a purely capitalistic system may not be the purest biblical economic program. God, as portrayed in the Bible, might have some other priorities in mind that capitalism does not address vigorously enough. (After issuing a second edition in 1984, IVP allowed the book to go out of print in 1989, mistakenly thinking it had completed its life cycle. Word Publishing picked up the publication and has successfully kept it in print, with 350,000 sold.) This book and John White's *The Golden Cow* were particularly nettlesome for IVCF president John Alexander. Problems with IVP critics caused him to say, "I believe there was never a board meeting when I was free of flak on this count." IVP defended to the administration and board "its policy of publishing thought-provoking literature without having to endorse everything in a book."

Those who are committed to the authority of Scripture still disagree on many issues regarding when war is appropriate, what the role of men and women in the church and home should be, how the end times will play out, and much more. So IVP published on all these topics, often using the four-views format pioneered by Robert Clouse (see

p. 69). The intention of doing this was to encourage readers to go back to Scripture, to look again and make sure they were hearing what God intended and not simply what their particular tradition was used to saying.

This was one feature of IVP's publishing philosophy in the United States that differentiated it from its sister publishing house in England. While IVP-UK consciously published to the center of its constituency, IVP-US, beginning under Jim Sire, consciously published to the breadth of its constituency. As a nondenominational publisher, IVP-US did not publish on strictly denominational matters but did publish on topics that were transdenominational and on which there was a range of opinions, such as divorce, sanctification and predestination. Nor did IVP feel it should only publish one brand of evangelical theology.

As a result, IVP-US occasionally published books that took opposite sides on issues where equally orthodox, Bible-believing Christians have disagreed. For example, Stott's *Baptism and Fullness of the Holy Spirit* did not view charismatic gifts in the same way that Charles Hummel's *Fire in the Fireplace* did. IVP's philosophy was that the best way to help resolve such disagreements was by open discussion, giving all an opportunity to make their best case from Scripture and let the Holy Spirit guide the result. IVP believes that open and free discussion guided by the Spirit is better than closing the issue prematurely and inadvertently settling on the wrong conclusion. This approach guided IVP's program regarding "openness theology" and other controversial issues.

other publishers. The debate captured the attention of many evangelical theologians and kept building into the following decade.

A third conversation in evangelicalism initiated by IVP was first brought to the attention of the editors in the early nineties by Rodney Clapp. Rodney always kept a careful eye on trends in culture and the church, helping to keep IVP current in its publishing program. He made the editorial team aware of the influence that postmodernism was likely to have in the culture broadly. Soon, he said, it would be important within the church as well.

Shortly thereafter Richard Middleton and Brian Walsh contacted IVP about doing a revised edition of their successful title *The Transforming Vision*, published in 1984, that would take account of the influence of postmodernism. When Rodney Clapp mentioned this to Andy Le Peau, Andy suggested it would be better for them to write an entirely new book. Rodney went back with the idea and the two readily agreed. Roger Olson commented on the result:

> Controversy over evangelical uses of postmodern philosophy began with the 1995 publication of *Truth Is Stranger Than It Used to Be* . . . by Canadian evangelical thinkers J. Richard Middleton and Brian J. Walsh. . . . Some evangelical critics felt they gave too much ground from under objective truth and accommodated too much to the relativistic spirit of the postmodern age. Sympathetic readers, however, discovered in *Truth Is Stranger Than It Used to Be* a refreshing departure from the conventional evangelical attacks on culture that are so often dependent on modern, Enlightenment modes of thinking.

True to form, IVP published not only books that looked favorably on some aspects of postmodernism but also those that strongly criticized it (such as *Truth Decay* by Douglas Groothuis and *Truth or Consequences* by Millard Erickson) as well as some that surveyed several views (*Christian Apologetics in a Postmodern World* and *Mapping Postmodernism*).

Significant academic publishing opportunities arose in arenas other than controversial ones. Frank Entwistle (who had succeeded Ronald Inchley as the head of IVP-UK) had made annual trips to the United States since the 1980s. In 1993 he visited Downers Grove, bringing with him a very attractive proposal that could help build IVP's reference program.

In 1953 IVP-UK had published the first edition of the *New Bible Commentary* (NBC); because IVP was tiny and had no capital, it was published in the United States by Eerdmans. Again in 1962 IVP-US was still so small that when the *New Bible Dictionary* (NBD) was published, Eerdmans again became the North American publisher. From first publication, IVP-US sold thousands of copies of both works to campus staff and InterVarsity students. Then in 1980 IVP-UK published the three-volume *Illustrated Bible Dictionary*. The U.S. rights for this project were bought by Tyndale House Publishers, and so the rights for the text-only version of the NBD went there as well, while the NBC stayed with Eerdmans.

In 1993 Entwistle said that IVP-UK wanted to consolidate those two works and the *New Bible Atlas* into the hands of one U.S. publisher and was opening up bidding. Since these books had originated with InterVarsity's

GENDER ISSUES

While IVP has tended to publish on both sides of issues about which evangelicals disagree, there have been some exceptions. For example, IVP tended not to publish much
from a dispensational perspective (a system of theology and the end times largely pop-
ularized by the Scofield Reference Bible) due to IVP's Reformed roots, its British heritage and the fact that there were plenty of popular and more academic dispensational
books published by others.

On the issue of men and women in the home, the church and society, IVP was generally more one-sided. Women held an equal place in the ministry of IVCF from the very
first, and many of IVP's first books were by women. As the discussion within evangelicalism about gender grew in the seventies and eighties, IVP published a four-views
book on the topic *(Women in Ministry)* and several books primarily about other issues
that also took a traditional viewpoint on women (for example, Ed Clowney's *The
Church* and Thomas Schreiner's *Paul, Apostle of God's Glory in Christ*).

IVP books wholly devoted to gender issues, however, generally supported so-
called egalitarian perspectives—books such as *Women, Authority and the Bible*
(1986), *Gender and Grace* (1990), *Women in the Church* (1995), and *Discovering Biblical Equality* (2004).

This was not always without controversy within IVP. In the mid-nineties a manuscript with a traditional (also called complementarian) perspective came before the
publishing committee and a vigorous disagreement erupted. Some in editorial and
marketing believed strongly that if IVP was to be an honest broker of evangelical ideas,
it should be willing to publish a responsible treatment like this. Others in editorial and
marketing believed strongly that publishing such a book was against IVP's ethos and
against IVP's prophetic calling to be a voice for justice. In addition, it was argued, publishing the book would undercut IVCF women campus staff who often struggled to be
accepted in their work by the broader evangelical community.

The controversy was tabled (the book was eventually published by another publisher) and not largely resolved until 2002 when Bob Fryling developed a "working
statement" with the department heads, including input from marketing and editorial.
The statement formally affirmed IVP's practice of continuing to publish four-views
books on the topic, and books on broader themes that include a variety of convictions
about men and women, while not publishing books whose major focus would under-
mine women in ministry within IVCF.

sister movement, and since IVP had distributed them for so long (mostly to the campus), they already seemed like part of the IVP line. Here was an opportunity to "bring them back home." It also fit strategically because Andy Le Peau and Dan Reid had decided a few years earlier that, although it would make perfect strategic sense to produce a one-volume Bible dictionary and commentary to solidify IVP's place as a significant reference publisher, there were too many good ones already out. It would also be hard to justify from a stewardship perspective.

Entwistle said that he would have to treat it as an open auction from all publishers. But after thorough analysis on their part, and seeing the progress IVP-US was making with its own reference program, IVP-UK concluded that their American counterparts were the best of all possible U.S. collaborators for them. Entwistle was impressed with the reference books Dan was beginning to churn out, with the *Dictionary of Jesus and the Gospels* having been published in 1992 (the first of four Gold Medallion-winning IVP New Testament dictionaries). Entwistle also saw how effectively IVP-US sold and marketed such books. So if Downers Grove could come up with the best offer, the British would be very pleased. That is just what happened, and the three volumes were published by IVP-US in 1994.

Not Entirely Fiction

While the push into more serious academic publishing proved successful, an attempt in the early 1990s to expand IVP's foray into fiction publishing did not fare as well. Books by Janette Oke and Frank Peretti had shown that there was a sustainable market for fiction. IVP had done some fiction in the seventies and eighties, such as the Archives of Anthropos series by John White, which did well due to his name recognition. But the optimum schedule for a fiction series called for releasing at least one new book a year instead one every three or four years as was the case for White. The success of *The Magic Bicycle* (1983) by John Bibee was followed up with sequels published annually beginning in 1987, and those were received well by an appreciative audience.

In 1993 IVP moved into fiction in earnest with the release of *The Beggar King* by Dan Hamilton (in the tradition and format of *The Singer*), *Stolen Identity* by Brian Regrut (a suspense thriller) and *The Forgotten Wiseman* by

John Timmerman (historical/biblical fiction). The next year Linda Shands's *A Time to Keep* (set in the Depression) was released. Each of these was the first of a series, and each had succeeding volumes released annually. But none of them caught hold in the Christian marketplace.

Were they, as in the case of *A Time to Keep*, too literary? Were they, as in the case of *Stolen Identity*, too gritty? Was the competition too great and IVP too late into the market? Did bookstores and readers think IVP was too sophisticated to appeal to average fiction readers? The only thing that was clear was that they sold poorly. Only the somewhat humorous *Spiritually Correct Bedtime Stories* (1995) by Chris Fabry and his two subsequent volumes could be counted successful. IVP decided shortly thereafter to leave fiction publishing to others.

From Main Street to Plaza Drive

One of the first things Ken DeRuiter had noticed when he arrived at IVP was the poor condition of the Main Street office. In the corner offices, when a door slammed, employees would hear plaster bits fall onto the windowsill. Herb Criley had made predictions about which piece of the building would fall off first! One Monday morning Nancy Fox came to her office only to discover that her bookshelves (laden with books, of course) had pulled out the anchors securing them to the wall, and all her books had come crashing down on her desk and on the chair where she would have been sitting had it happened during the week.

When author Jim Conway visited IVP and spoke at an office meeting, he said with wry humor, "I feel really welcomed here at IVP. I see you've put new tape on the carpet just for my visit!" (Of course, that wasn't the case at all. New brown tape was applied to the fraying brown carpet quite regularly!)

In addition, the typesetting room often had its own private waterfall when it rained. The typesetters covered machines with plastic, and on occasion Marj Sire actually worked while holding an umbrella! Sometimes they vacuumed up the water several times a day.

The building had many charming features, of course. The "dungeon," as the basement was known, was used for storage until the damp and mildew made that totally impractical. Nonetheless, employees would brave the musty air and tiny streams of water during tornado warnings. It was a great bonding time, but some wondered if the tornado wouldn't be a better fate.

The car elevator was no doubt unique to office facilities in the western suburbs of Chicago. It was so old that the last repairman was a retired eighty-year-old gentleman who could not think of anyone else to recommend to maintain and repair it when he called it quits in 1990. So Arnold Young learned to grease the hydraulic lift himself. There were plenty of drums full of oil in the basement just for this purpose. They had been left when IVP bought the building in 1970. Arnold prayed regularly that the elevator would not break.

Some employees didn't like working in the building at night because the elevator would clink and clang and shake unexpectedly as temperatures changed. Once Kathy Burrows got stuck in the elevator (which she used to get between floors when she was recovering from a broken foot) and had to have help getting out. Once the evening cleaning crew got stuck in the elevator when they couldn't undo the latch that opened the doors to the second floor. The next morning Arnold heard them banging and let them out!

The building was packed with offices, cubicles and desks. People were squeezed in wherever possible. The layout was a maze of narrow halls, inconveniently laid out, with people who worked together often located on different floors or different sides of the building. Kathy Burrows's office actually had two doors that allowed people to get from one side of the building to the other. She didn't mind, she said. In fact, she enjoyed the stimulation this "hallway" provided. But many feared to use that route.

Every space was utilized. The master file of books (holding one copy of every printing of every title) had outgrown the shelving in Jim Hoover's office and now also occupied a wall in Kathy Burrows's space. Filing cabinets lined hallways.

Ken was set on making a change. He worked with Jim Hagen, Nancy Fox and IVCF board members Don Powell and Don Bodel to study the options to buy, lease or build. Ultimately, in April 1994, IVP broke ground on the side lawn next to the distribution center in Westmont. When Jim Nyquist had arranged for the purchase of this piece of land, he had envisioned the possibility of an office building there someday alongside the warehouse.

Five architectural firms had been interviewed for the job in 1993. Four of them said, in essence, "Here's what we can do for you." They thought they had great things to offer. The fifth, Ware and Associates, said, "What would you like us to do for you?" It was immediately clear that they were a company that would listen and that they were the right fit for IVP's collaborative office culture. In fact, Ware and Associates spent several days at the Main Street building interviewing almost all employees about how they worked and what their needs were. Lots of light, lots of work surfaces and lots of bookshelves were asked for and designed into the building. (In fact, those supplying the office furniture said they had never had an order for so many bookshelves in any building they had ever worked on!)

The department heads made clear to the firm that IVP was a publisher and not a church, so the building should not look like a church. But the architects were able to design a beautiful hallway under a skylight that was reminiscent of a cloister in an abbey and suitable for a modern scriptorium. Near the entrance a "bookstore" was located to make a clear statement to those first entering the building that IVP is about books and loves books. It also functioned as a place to sell books to the occasional retail

The skylight at 430 Plaza Drive gave the main hallway (here decorated for Christmas) and the whole office a warm, bright, indoor courtyard effect.

customer who stopped by and for employees to get books needed for authors or promotion without disturbing the distribution center's inventory.

Ware and Associates also tied the building to the publishing industry by designing a horizontal look on the exterior with colored mullions between the windows representing pages of a book lying on its side. The colors used in design of the building were also modifications of the colors used in full-color printing: red, yellow, blue and black. The red, yellow and blue were found on the hallway walls, in conference rooms, on the exterior of the windows and in the carpeting. The black was represented in the gray tone that dominates the wall color.

In January 1995 Jim Hagen supervised a smooth weekend move to 430 Plaza Drive. Now the DC crew didn't have to drive several miles to an office meeting, and office folks had books instantly available, rather than having to wait for the next trip across town. Everyone enjoyed the clean, efficient space.

Access to the Internet and to e-mail also came with the building (an IVP first as well) thanks to the work of Ron Lanier, Andy Shermer and others. One of the few problems with the new building occurred when the office of *Journal of Christian Nursing* editor Melodee Yohe flooded! Apparently a worker had punctured a PVC drain, which ran from the roof down the inside wall, when he was screwing in the strips that held the bookshelves.

In laying out the floor plan, Nancy and others were careful to work with the architects to overcome the obviously inconvenient layout of the Main Street office. Those departments that interacted most often were located next to each other. Since editorial interfaced most frequently with Nancy's team (typesetting, design and production), those two departments were put side by side. Marketing had frequent interaction with Nancy's department as well as business. So it was placed with production on one side and business on the other. The plan worked so well, in fact, that a few months into the new office, employees began to complain that they didn't see each other as often and felt a bit isolated. And that was true. On Main Street, to visit anyone meant one ended up seeing almost everyone on the way. Now that rarely happened. The advent of e-mail amplified this trend since employees could now send letters, manuscripts or other messages over the network (even to coworkers next door) instead of hand delivering them.

One feature of the Main Street office that frustrated Nancy and Arnold was its electrical wiring. Arnold had to buy large boxes of fuses to replace those that blew out frequently. That was especially a problem when Nancy Iglesias and Sue Bielat organized a "waffle-rama." Circuits were blown all over the building when a dozen people plugged in their waffle irons for an officewide party. So Nancy Fox made sure the new office kitchen was equipped so that each outlet was on a different circuit to allow future waffle-ramas to go unimpeded.

The new building's design also included the "Blue Chair Room," a nook near the restrooms. A large, stuffed, blue recliner had been brought into the Main Street building by HIS editor Paul Fromer in the late sixties because he had back trouble and needed a comfortable place to think and plan. His successor, Steve Board, didn't want it, and so it ended up in Ralph Gates's office until it migrated to a corner of the first floor, between the steel racks of bulk book storage. Often, employees who weren't feeling well, but who weren't sure they were sick enough to go home, would go down to that quiet corner for a few minutes to rest in the blue chair. A pillow and blanket were soon added. The architects preserved this tradition, and Fromer's original blue chair was installed in its own little room on Plaza Drive, where it still resides.

One day, a year or so after the move, no one could find Greg Metzger, the campus and academic sales manager. No one had seen him leave the building. He was paged by the receptionist, Audrey Ward, but he did not respond. It was only late in the afternoon, as everyone was leaving for the day, that a sleepy, bleary-eyed Greg emerged from the Blue Chair Room. He had inadvertently fallen asleep in the dark quiet of the room after lunch.

Another personal touch to the building was added by the typesetters. They placed bird feeders in the courtyard outside their window to welcome all their feathered friends who had been threatened by Herb Criley on Main Street a decade before (see p. 89).

The new facility was celebrated at an open house on April 7, 1995. Many former employees were invited, along with friends from key printing partners such as the Banta Corporation and those from nearby publishing houses such as Scripture Press, Tyndale House Publishers and Christianity Today, Inc. Then on June 2 the building was dedicated in a liturgy created by the staff that included President Steve Hayner of InterVarsity Christian Fellowship and Board Chair Tom Boyle. The singing of "Take My Life and Let It Be" and "Who Is on the Lord's Side?" augmented the prayers of dedication that were read in turn by members of the IVCF board, IVCF leaders, IVP leaders and members of each department.

As the architects knew, space and the way it is designed affect people. They wanted to create a working environment that people enjoyed being in, especially since they would spend such a large percentage of their lives there. And their goals were fulfilled. But the new building also marked something of a transition of IVP from a "family" operation (without a literal family owning the business) to a more corporate identity. A new corporate logo was introduced as the new building was occupied (with three swashes placed prominently above the lowercase letters "ivp," see p. 146). E-mail and the floor plan made the office more efficient. IVP author and theologian Stan Grenz even joked with the editors about the significance of moving "from Main Street to Plaza Drive." Wasn't that a metaphor, he asked tongue in cheek, for moving from the heartland to the corporate world? Perhaps that was a bit overstated, but there was an element of truth in it.

What happened to 5206 Main Street? It was sold to Sievers Construction, which transformed it into Founders Hill Brewing Company, a micro-

Moving the office from Downers Grove to Westmont reunited the distribution and warehousing operation with the rest of IVP.

brewery and restaurant. (Founders Hill later went out of business and was replaced by Emmett's Ale House.) The building was gutted and huge brewing vats were installed on the first floor where office meetings had been held. The vats were so tall that they extended to the upper floor where offices had been. That meant, of course, that something was still brewing in Jim Sire's office!

To the Future Through the Past

Sometimes what a publisher doesn't publish is just as important as what it does publish. Over the years Dan Reid and Andy Le Peau had given long thought to what was needed to complete the reference program. Once Dan commented to Andy, "If we are to be seen as a major player, one of the obvious things we need to do is publish a critical commentary series." This would send a clear signal about IVP's seriousness as a publisher in this arena. Yet several such series were already in progress, including two strong series from other evangelical publishers. So with some regret, but not much, they said no, as they had done with a Bible dictionary, to what was strategically obvious but questionable from a stewardship perspective.

But when theologian Tom Oden contacted IVP in 1995 at the suggestion of Christopher Hall about the Ancient Christian Commentary on Scripture (ACCS), Dan and Andy immediately saw its originality and the breadth of impact the project could have not only on the scholarly community but on the church as a whole. Andy commented to Dan, "This is why we said no to doing a critical commentary series—so we would have the time and resources available to devote to this much more important project."

Oden was a scholar of no little stature, respected in a wide variety of ecumenical venues. His three-volume *Systematic Theology*, published from 1987 to 1992, was recognized as a unique effort to call the church back to its roots, to measure the present by means of the past. While largely an evangelical publisher, InterVarsity Press, for historical reasons, never rested entirely easily within the American brand of evangelicalism. Oden's own self-identification as orthodox, ecumenical and evangelical was actually quite close to the way InterVarsity Press saw itself.

Dan also saw synergy with the Oden proposal because of IVP's ties with the college ministry. When the proposal for the ACCS arrived at IVP, the first indications were coming in from the campus of a deep longing among students (who often came from unstable backgrounds) for something that felt permanent and lasting. Just one indicator was the unlikely popularity

---

HOW DID ODEN THINK OF THAT?

In the late 1980s Tom Oden received in the mail an offer from a publisher for a set of commentaries from the church fathers, with excerpts arranged by the books of the Bible. For $390 this handsome collection of volumes would be his. He immediately sent in his money, only to discover later (as did many others, when the volumes never arrived) that the entire thing was a scam. There was no such series. There was no such publisher. And he would never see his $390 again. (The perpetrator was eventually convicted of mail fraud.) Tom was so distressed that he determined that such a series should actually be created and offered to the public. The result was the ACCS.

The episode recalls the words of Joseph to his brothers at the end of the book of Genesis when they were terrified that he might act in a vengeful manner because of the way they had treated him when he was younger: "You meant evil against me; but God meant it for good" (Gen 50:20 RSV).

Commenting on this verse, as quoted in the ACCS volume *Genesis 12—50,* Chrysostom wrote,

> See how great a thing virtue is, how powerful and invincible, and how profound the weakness of evil. . . . Hence Paul also said, "For those who love God all things work together for good." "All things," he says. What is meant by "all things"? Opposition and apparent disappointment—even these things are turned into good, which is exactly what happened with this remarkable man.

What a con artist saw as a means to a fast buck was redeemed into an effort that has nurtured the whole church.

---

of the music of *Chant* from the Benedictine Monks of Santo Domingo de Silos, released in 1994, which sold six million copies worldwide.

Having agreed to join together in this project, the team began facing a number of challenges. First, what should the volumes look like? What size? What layout? One model was the beautiful but costly Steinsaltz edition of the Talmud that was then appearing, volume by volume. Oden had

The Ancient Christian Commentary on Scripture signaled the renewed importance of the early church for evangelicals and gained a wide audience among Catholic and Orthodox readers as well.

a desire to somehow give a nod to *glossa ordinaria,* a sacred text artfully surrounded with authoritative comment and insight. How could this be done without increasing the typesetting costs enormously and without confusing contemporary readers who would not have seen such a format before? Even with the somewhat simplified layout that was settled on with art director Kathy Burrows, typesetters were not able to utilize automatic footnote placement, adding to the time and cost of each volume. Everyone agreed that Kathy gave the series an elegant look.

Another complicating factor regarded revisions and corrections of manuscripts. Normally, an editor and author work together on a book as partners. For the ACCS a general editor and the ACCS editorial support team at Drew University were added to the mix. Finally, in 1998, *Mark* and *Romans,* the first two ACCS volumes, were released. It took some time, after a half-dozen volumes, to work out smoothly which responsibilities were to be handled in New Jersey and which in Illinois. In addition, as with any multivolume, multicontributor work, volume editors worked at different speeds, sometimes to the consternation of the general editor and the publisher.

Don Stephenson's vision for direct mail was instrumental in laying the groundwork for the excellent sales results of the ACCS. During his years at Word Publishing in Texas, he had seen how successful direct mail programs had been there. So he was anxious to build up the IVP Book Club. When his colleague at Word, Steve Gibson, quit to go into business for himself as a direct mail consultant, Don brought him on board as a consultant to bring a new level of expertise to IVP some years before the ACCS appeared.

Early on, Steve encouraged IVP to expand beyond the Book Club by offering continuity programs in 1994 for the Bible Speaks Today Series and the IVP New Testament Commentary Series. Those who signed up would receive a new commentary every couple months. The CIS publishing software that IVP used was not adequate to handle the needs of a continuity program, so a separate stand-alone system had to be brought in, the two being integrated manually. The work on these programs gave IVP a base of experience that set the stage for the success of the ACCS direct mail program in 1998.

Subscribers to the series could collect all the volumes at a guaranteed discount and receive a free copy of *Reading Scripture with the Church Fathers* by Christopher Hall, associate series editor for the ACCS. Over the next six years, more than 1.25 million solicitations were sent out by mail. Twenty thousand people signed up, with about ten thousand staying on for all the volumes. It became IVP's most successful program of its kind and proved instrumental in IVP's financial viability in the next few years.

In addition, the series showed that IVP was able to reach effectively into Catholic and Orthodox markets for the first time while proving that the evangelical world was also ready to hear what the ancient fathers of the church had to say. The project put IVP on a new plane. The editor of the journal *Books and Culture,* John Wilson, called it "the most important project in religious publishing at the end of the second millennium."

The DeRuiter Years Close

One of Ken DeRuiter's initiatives was to get IVP into Bible publishing. Ken knew how well Bibles sold in his stores and thought IVP should be part of this. After many discussions about a variety of options, a study Bible based on LifeGuides was settled on. Ken, Andy and Don met with folks at Zondervan and obtained permission to use the NIV text. Bible study editor Cindy Bunch developed sample studies, and many in editorial, marketing, production and design gave input to the format and layout of the project. Focus groups were also employed to give input to the whole product idea. Cindy then signed up writers to fill in studies that were not already in print in the LifeGuide series, and in 1994 *The NIV Quiet Time Bible: New Testament and Psalms* was successfully released. Two years later the full Bible came out, providing a study program that would take one through the Scriptures in two years.

Though the New Testament version and the whole-Bible version both sold well, they did not continue selling at a pace that allowed economical reprinting. With the intense competition of many Bible editions being offered from many publishers, and without an entire line of Bibles to offer to the public that would allow for ongoing promotion, IVP decided not to pursue Bibles further.

In April 1995 IVP became one of the first Christian publishers to go into cyberspace, launching its website with nine other Christian organizations as a charter member of Gospelcom.net. Sally Sampson was one of those most excited about this new technology, championing the role it could play in publicity and promotion for IVP. Given her role in copywriting in the marketing department, it was natural for her to be appointed as webmaster.

Don Stephenson required that when the site launched, each of IVP's eight hundred titles would have its own page—an enormous task that daunted Sally. At the time Mark Gates, a computer science major at the University of Illinois and the son of former IVP director of marketing Ralph Gates, was working temporarily in the distribution center. Andy Shermer suggested to

Jim Hagen that Mark move over to help with the Web project, and it was so. Within three weeks Mark had magically created all the webpages Don called for. By the end of the year, the site was receiving over 60,000 hits a month. By the end of the decade that figure had grown tenfold.

When the website was launched mid-decade, it was still largely a mystery to most customers (and most IVP employees). One day an employee reported to Andy Le Peau that someone had seen pornography on the IVP website. Andy asked Sally Sampson if someone could have hacked into IVP's website somehow. Sally was mystified when she could find nothing amiss.

A few days later she tracked down the problem. Andy Shermer had encouraged IVP staff to get comfortable with the new software by surfing around the IVP website. So Marj Sire did just that, starting at IVP's home page, which among other things mentioned the people who had built the site and how to contact them. From there she linked to Mark Gates's personal homepage. From that page she linked to a University of Illinois website directory. From there she clicked to another student's website (someone Mark didn't know) and from there to some rather vulgar stuff! Later that day she told a coworker of her surprise to see such horrible things "on IVP's website," not realizing she had left IVP's website many clicks before!

While sales in Bible studies and reference books grew strong and steady, IVP's Saltshaker Books continued to struggle. The vision had been to create a line of books that took on issues in a substantive but largely narrative fashion that would appeal to a wide lay readership. With Leighton Ford's story of his son, *Sandy,* as a model, Don Stephenson developed books like Sis Levin's story of her husband's kidnapping in Lebanon, *Beirut Diary,* and *In Sickness and in Health,* the story of a man who left his gay lifestyle, became a Christian and died of AIDS shortly after getting married.

As other books in the line were released, with most selling modestly, management learned its lesson and reprinted far more cautiously, limited advertising and started releasing books more often in paperback rather than hardback. More emphasis was given to topical books than narratives. New titles included *Don't Miss Your Kids!* by Charlene Baumbich (1991), *Sexual Harassment No More* by Jim and Sally Conway (1993) and a series of five "50 Ways" books coauthored by Gordon Aeschliman and Tony Campolo (1991-1993). Despite these changes, the results were mixed.

Some books did well, but many struggled to meet expectations without authors who had strong platforms from which to promote their sales.

IVP did have a heritage to build on: many successful books for ordinary Christian readers, from *How to Give Away Your Faith* to *The Fight* to *Out of the Saltshaker*. But Le Peau had underestimated how the competition from

FIFTY YEARS OF PUBLISHING

In 1997 IVP celebrated its fiftieth anniversary and soon thereafter produced an attractive poster showing some of the most significant books it has published. The poster said, "For over 50 years InterVarsity Press has been providing scholarly, biblically balanced books for Christians who long to serve God with their minds as well as their hearts. Today we look ahead with a commitment to build on that foundation of excellence, providing substantive, challenging and engaging reading for thoughtful Christians in the 21st century." The books listed on the poster were:

1954 *My Heart—Christ's Home,* Robert Boyd Munger

1958 *Basic Christianity,* John R. W. Stott

1966 *How to Give Away Your Faith,* Paul Little

1968 *Know Why You Believe,* Paul Little

1968 *The God Who Is There,* Francis A. Schaeffer

1968 *Escape from Reason,* Francis A. Schaeffer

1973 *Knowing God,* J. I. Packer

1975 *The Singer,* Calvin Miller

1976 *The Fight,* John White

1976 *The Universe Next Door,* James W. Sire

1979 *Out of the Saltshaker,* Rebecca Manley Pippert

1980 *A Long Obedience in the Same Direction,* Eugene H. Peterson

1986 *The Cross of Christ,* John R. W. Stott

1986 *Jesus: Lord and Savior,* F. F. Bruce (part of The Jesus Library)

1986 *Foundations of the Christian Faith,* James Montgomery Boice

1988 *Too Busy Not to Pray,* Bill Hybels

1991 *Darwin on Trial,* Phillip E. Johnson

1998 *Mark* (first volume of Ancient Christian Commentary on Scripture), Thomas C. Oden, general editor

1999 *The Challenge of Jesus,* N. T. Wright

other Christian publishers in this field had grown through the eighties, and he had overestimated IVP's ability to change its image. Even in its popular books, there was a thoughtfulness, a serious-mindedness that undergirded them. The editorial team was predisposed to contract such books, the marketing team knew and appreciated them, and the market was used to seeing them in IVP's catalogs. There was a limitation, however, to how many of these books could gain a wide readership. The time, money and change of mentality required to make them successful was a higher price than IVP could pay.

What Ronald Inchley, the first publications secretary (that is, publisher) of IVP in England, wrote about his situation in the forties, IVP in the United States might have paid more attention to in the eighties and nineties: "As the work expanded after the war there was always the temptation to move across into more general Christian publishing. Authors for such books would not be so difficult to find, and, with a wider market for the books, the financial return would be quicker and greater. But these temptations were resisted."

During 1995 it became increasingly clear that Ken DeRuiter's medical condition was preventing him from functioning at full capacity. (Later he was diagnosed with Alzheimer's disease.) So on January 31, 1996, he announced that he was stepping down for medical reasons. Barney Ford, IVCF vice president, became acting executive director and initiated a search for a new director. That summer at the CBA convention, Ken, who had made many friends in the industry over the years, was honored with the Chairperson's Award of the ECPA for his contributions as a bookseller, as head of InterVarsity Press and as an ECPA/ECPO Board member.

The years leading up to Ken's departure had been difficult for the department heads: Nancy Fox, Jim Hagen, Andy Le Peau and Don Stephenson. With Ken operating at less than full capacity (though it was not clear why at the time), a leadership vacuum slowly opened. Each department head wanted the Press to move forward and not to suffer any setbacks, but each had a slightly different view of which direction to go and how to get there. Which markets should be pursed? What kinds of books served the mission best? What was the mission? How should IVP view its relationship with IVCF—as an asset, as a burden, as a partnership or not? Was the spir-

Ken DeRuiter and his team gather in his office at the end of his IVP tenure. (l. to r.) Nancy Fox (production and fulfillment), Don Stephenson (sales and marketing), Jim Hagen (business and finance), Wai-Chin Matsuoka (assistant to the executive director), Ken DeRuiter (executive director) and Andy Le Peau (editorial).

ituality of the office culture an asset or a liability? How could IVP recapture its success of the seventies with books like the bestsellers of that era—*The Fight, Knowing God, The Singer, Rich Christians in an Age of Hunger* and others? The natural tensions that exist between any editorial department (concerned primarily about content) and any marketing department (concerned primarily about sales) intensified. There was no clear leadership to guide the team through these important and difficult questions, and so there was a tendency for departments to act separately.

As the search for a permanent replacement for Ken took place, IVP celebrated its fiftieth anniversary. At mid-life there was much to look back on with pride and satisfaction. Yet concerns lingered about identity, purpose, ethos and the future.

The Fryling Years Begin

The Late Nineties

"What Jesus did was not a mere example of something else, not a mere manifestation of some larger truth; it was itself the climactic event and fact of cosmic history. From then on everything is different. Do not put all the eschatological weight on that which is still to come. The whole point of New Testament Christianity is that the End came forward into the present in Jesus the Messiah."

N. T. WRIGHT, THE CHALLENGE OF JESUS, 1999

In March 1997, Steve Hayner, president of IVCF, announced that Bob Fryling (an IVCF vice president living in Madison) was appointed IVP executive director (his title later changing to publisher). Bob had joined IVCF campus staff in New England in 1969 after graduating from Drexel University, where he had been an active student leader in InterVarsity. He became area director three years after that and was then promoted to eastern regional director in 1975. He and his wife, Alice, published their first book with IVP in 1978, *A Handbook for Engaged Couples,* which has sold over 300,000 copies and is still in print. In 1981 he was appointed director of

Shortly after moving into 430 Plaza Drive, the employees of InterVarsity Press gathered in front of the building's main entrance.

campus ministries for the nation, served as director of human resources in 1983, and again was appointed director of campus ministries in 1984, taking on the additional role of vice president two years later.

Bob came to IVP with two decades of administrative experience and interpersonal skills, including that of supervising a diverse staff of several hundred spread across the country. While his strong ties to the Fellowship were clear, he also came as a published author and someone who loved books and ideas. In addition, he had a heart full of emotion for people and God's work in the world. It was not uncommon to see tears come to his eyes as he spoke at an office meeting about these things.

Personnel Moves

In autumn 1997, Don Stephenson announced he was leaving to join Family University in San Diego. IVP's collaborative culture then went into high gear. Employees suggested names to Bob Fryling for a replacement, and candidates were interviewed not just by the top brass but by the entire marketing and sales department as well. One candidate suggested by sales manager Jim Connon was Jeff Crosby, who took the job Bob offered him.

Jeff had owned and operated his own Logos Bookstore in Bloomington, Indiana, before becoming executive director of the Association of Logos Bookstores. In the previous two years he had been a vice president at Ingram/Spring Arbor distributors (which was IVP's number one customer). Jeff's first day on the job was total immersion into the InterVarsity culture at the National Staff Conference, held at the Chicago Hyatt O'Hare in January 1998. His slight disorientation in that setting was relieved somewhat with the celebration of IVP's fiftieth anniversary at a plenary session one evening, including an enjoyable ten-minute video produced by IVCF's multimedia division, Twentyonehundred Productions.

Jeff was also a lover of books and was one of the best-read marketing

BOOKS BY INTERVARSITY STAFF

IVP has had a long heritage of publishing books by IV campus staff workers, its very first homegrown publication being written by Jane Hollingsworth (see chap. 1). The emphasis on Bible study, evangelism and multiethnicity that is found in the campus ministry has shone through the publishing program over the years.

The first IVP books originating in the United States were Bible study guides written by staff. And when it came time to launch the LifeGuide series, IVP turned to many staff and former staff to author a number of volumes. These included Jim Hoover, Andy and Phyllis Le Peau, Andrea Sterk, Pete Scazzero, Don Baker, Steve Eyre, Jack Kuhatschek, Bill Syrios, Bob Hunter and others.

Evangelism, another emphasis within InterVarsity's campus ministry, also spawned a number of books. *How to Give Away Your Faith* and *Know Why You Believe* by Paul Little were of immense help to Christians in explaining the gospel to others and became bestsellers in the 1960s. Rebecca Manley Pippert (who had been on staff in the Northwest) followed in Paul Little's footsteps with her own classic on evangelism, *Out of the Saltshaker*. Kentucky Area Director Mack Stiles in 1995 provided another updated approach to witness with his *Speaking of Jesus*. In 1999 Don Everts, on staff in Colorado and still in his twenties, published *Jesus with Dirty Feet*, aimed at postmodern students, which became a standard evangelistic giveaway for the campus work and many churches, including Willow Creek Community Church.

What had been a trickle soon became a steady stream. Rick Richardson from northern Illinois offered new paradigms in *Evangelism Outside the Box,* published in 2000. Will Metzger, long-time staff from Delaware, revised his classic text from a distinctly Reformed perspective, *Tell the Truth,* in 2002. John Teter from southern California offered his own motivational book on evangelism with *Get the Word Out* (2003).

It was InterVarsity staff who also helped populate IVP's publishing program with books from multiethnic perspectives such as Carl Ellis's *Free at Last?* for African Americans, the team-written *Following Jesus Without Dishonoring Your Parents* for Asian Americans, *Being Latino in Christ* by Orlando Crespo and *Being White* for the rest who maybe didn't know they were ethnic too.

Jim Sire led the way for books authored by IVP employees. Some publishers thought it best to avoid potential conflicts of interest by adopting a policy whereby employees were specifically prohibited from publishing with the house they worked for. IVP successfully managed to walk this tightrope of accepting some and rejecting others from in-house authors, the results being a number of high-quality books. Editors Drew Blankman, Cindy Bunch, Rodney Clapp, Ruth Goring, Jim Hoover, Al Hsu, Dan Reid and David Zimmerman and others all saw their names gracing the covers of IVP books. In addition, Mark Smith, who started working in the design department in 1998, wrote, at the suggestion of Cindy Bunch, the very successful *Tolkien's Ordinary Virtues* and followed this up with *Aslan's Call.*

All these and dozens more staff-written books were gifts from InterVarsity to the broader church, gifts of creative insights, tested methods and biblical commitments that had shaped the movement over the decades.

folks in the industry. He not only loved good books in general, he thoroughly enjoyed IVP's brand of publishing in particular. Stepping into a department that felt the absence of Don's expansive personality, Jeff provided the team a steady, quiet and effective pace. He was well connected to many key people in the industry as well—authors, publishers, bookstore owners. All these proved to be assets to IVP in the coming years. He brought in Phyllis Tickle from the religion desk at *Publishers Weekly* to let the whole sales and marketing team pick her brain and hear her always penetrating insights about publishing and the world of faith.

At staff conference in 1998 Sally Sampson gave Jeff another kind of orientation. She introduced her dream of creating a subdepartment of sales and marketing devoted to developing and designing all the materials IVP needed to promote and sell its books. It would combine the talents of copywriters and designers, who could benefit from the synergy such a team would create, with input from an experienced designer like Kathy Burrows. Jeff, being new, was aware that he didn't have enough context to

FAMILY CONNECTIONS

Maybe one reason IVP had such a family feel was that often more than one member of a family worked there. Jim and Marj Sire were one of the first couples to work as full-time employees at IVP. Steve Palmer headed up data processing in the early eighties, and his wife, Darcy, worked in editorial both in rights and as an administrative assistant. In the early nineties Rhonda Skinner handled rights and permissions while her husband, Kevin, worked in accounting. Dick Ecker worked as a data processing consultant in the eighties and his wife, Myrna, helped out in office services. Al Hsu had jobs in several departments while his wife, Ellen, joined IVP in 1997 as rights coordinator, later becoming rights manager. Andy Shermer worked in information services while his wife, Holly, handled returns in the distribution center. After Rebecca Vorwerk (creative services) married Jeff Larson in 2005, he also started working at the distribution center.

But there have been more than just husband and wife teams. In the sixties and seventies, Wilma Holmes headed up distribution and warehousing, while her daughter Nora ran typesetting. Shirley Peska joined the production department in 1985, a few years before her daughter, Deborah Kaiser, worked in marketing. Paul Keenon took charge of the distribution center several years before his sister, Kathy Carlson, started at IVP in 1984. Although Ralph Gates left in 1985, his daughter Heather was an assistant in the production department from 1994-1996, and his son Mark worked in information services from 2000-2004. Sisters Allison and Lisa Rieck both joined the editorial department. IVP was careful in all of these situations to make sure family members didn't supervise one another.

IVP also has had its share of office romances. Gene Eble (editorial) and Diane Fila-kowsky (production) overlapped from 1978-1981 at IVP before getting married. Jack Kuhatschek (editorial) and Sandy Loder (marketing) met in 1982 and were married a few years later. Andrew Craft (information services) married Sally Sampson (creative services) in 1999. The two of them met four years earlier when Andrew started at IVP. He was brother of design assistant Amy Craft (1988-1992) who later married the son of typesetter Gail Munroe.

Nancy/David

make a quick decision on such a major shift. He didn't have to worry, however. It would not be the last time Sally would raise it.

By the end of the 1998 Nancy Fox was engaged to former IVCF board member David Scott and was about to move to Atlanta. So Anne Gerth (who attended First Presbyterian Church in Downers Grove along with Nancy) was hired in November 1998 to replace her. Anne brought experience in organizational training and development—and a decisive personality that filled the gap Nancy had left.

While neither Anne nor Jeff had direct InterVarsity experience in their backgrounds, both had many IV-connected friends and found IVP's combination of spiritual vitality and focus on business a comfortable one. The professional sensibilities that both brought to IVP helped keep employees accountable while not losing the importance placed on personal relationships. Soon they partnered to offer an intensive training program in customer service for those in all departments who had most direct contact with customers. Anne's experience as an operations manager had its effect as well, typified by the training she offered in interviewing prospective employees and in small ways such as the upgrading of the quality and character of Christmas gifts for employees and authors.

Robert A. Fryling, shown here in 1999, joined IVP in 1997 after serving in InterVarsity Christian Fellowship's campus ministry division in various capacities, starting in 1969.

Bob Fryling also brought his own brand of professionalism and financial savvy to IVP. His was a managerial sense honed by both the American Management Association and the Fuller Institute of Organizational Development. Bob led leadership training programs for middle-level IVP employees and office discussions of the bestselling business book *Good to Great*.

In addition, Bob provided decades of experience in InterVarsity (which quite deliberately was often referred to by employees as "The Fellowship"). He worked hard to create a warm, inclusive family feel through his announcements, reflections and news offered at the biweekly office meetings, and going to lunch in small groups with everyone in the office. In these and other ways he sought to bring all the departments into a sense of unity rather than allow them to remain isolated groups that were sometimes at odds with one another. Jeff noticed immediately the contrast between IVP and his previous employer, where managers were frowned on for eating lunch with people who were not at their organizational level. With the installation of a strong leader like Bob, who had clear ties to the rest of the movement, the questions that had dogged IVP's leadership in the early nineties began to be answered.

The department-head team had transitioned significantly in just a couple years. Two were new and came without significant InterVarsity background (Gerth and Crosby). Two were long-term employees who had had much InterVarsity experience before coming to IVP (Le Peau and Hagen). Fryling was a mix of both—being new to IVP but having been with InterVarsity long-term. This combination gave the IVP leadership team a sense of history and a grasp of the trajectory IVP was following along with fresh perspectives and ideas.

Transitions continued when Rodney Clapp left IVP and began working as editor of *Prism* in 1999 (later moving to Baker to form the Brazos imprint). His wide range of reading, network of relationships and incisive thinking had contributed much in his nearly ten years at IVP. He had, for example, first highlighted the importance of the "Yale School" of postliberals for IVP and worked with Timothy Phillips and Dennis Okholm to make that the theme of the 1995 Wheaton Theology Conference (the second of a series that IVP continues to cosponsor with the Wheaton College Graduate School). The result was *The Nature of Confession*. He also encouraged IVP to continue to embrace a wider circle of authors, seeing much common cause and helpful perspectives with those of a broadly orthodox and sympathetic evangelical persuasion. He, for example, was the one who first brought Tom Oden into contact with IVP, resulting in the publication of

Two Worlds, which paved the way for IVP's work with Oden on the important Ancient Christian Commentary on Scripture.

Gary Deddo was hired to replace Rodney as an academic editor specializing in theology. He had worked for twenty years with IVCF, half in undergraduate work in California and half with graduate ministry in New Jersey. Gary found time to earn his Ph.D. in systematic theology from the University of Aberdeen in Scotland under James Torrance in between these two stints. One of the IVP authors happiest to hear that Gary was on board was Phillip Johnson, the author of *Darwin on Trial.* The two had met at Princeton where Gary was working with InterVarsity and Phillip was speaking on evolution. Their collaboration on future books looked promising.

A significant book for IVP emerged at the end of the decade during the "Following Christ, Shaping Our World" conference—a first-of-its-kind gathering cosponsored by the Graduate and Faculty Ministries of IVCF and InterVarsity Press. Held during five days straddling 1998 and 1999 at the Chicago Hilton and Towers, the conference brought together about fifteen hundred graduate students, faculty and mentors to consider how to think, work and live as Christians in a variety of professions and academic disciplines.

New Testament scholar Tom (N. T.) Wright, author of many books, including the highly acclaimed 1997 release *Jesus and the Victory of God,* gave four plenary addresses that provided the backbone of the conference. During the meetings, Dan Reid and Andy Le Peau met with Tom on more than one occasion to discuss possible writing projects, but none clicked with Tom. Wright described the setting this way:

On January 2, 1999 (my parents' 52nd wedding anniversary, as it happens), Chicago had its worst snowstorm in over thirty years. All day the blizzard raged, shutting major highways and bringing suburban life to a near standstill. For the previous three days I had been able to see the lakeshore from my hotel window only two blocks away; now I could scarcely see the other side of the street.

That evening, as the snowplows struggled around the streets and the airline phones were jammed with callers transferring from canceled flights, I gave my fourth and final address at a remarkable conference.

After the address, Tom, Andy and Dan met with Brian Walsh, an old friend of Tom's from their days together in Toronto and coauthor of two IVP books. Brian suggested that Tom take the four lectures and create out of them an introduction to his thought on Jesus. The idea was for a book that did not require the scholarly heft needed for one to work through the several thousand pages of writing planned for Tom's multivolume work Christian Origins and the Question of God.

Tom immediately latched on to the idea and the four (stranded by the storm) talked late into the night over liquid refreshments about the possibility of getting such a book out in short order. Within a few months Tom, one of the fastest pens in the Western world, had completed the manuscript, adding four additional chapters to the original four lectures. In October 1999 *The Challenge of Jesus* was published—a book that fulfilled its role as a key introduction to the central thought of one of the leading biblical scholars of the day.

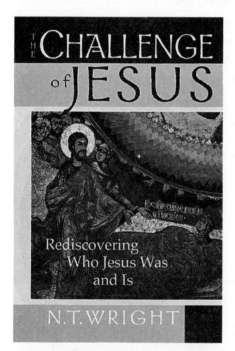

The Challenge of Jesus became a key book introducing a wide range of readers to N. T. Wright's thought on the life and work of Jesus, which was having a major impact on the scholarly world.

It was at that same conference that Jim Sire officially celebrated his retirement from InterVarsity. His contribution to the Fellowship and to the wider church was recognized from the platform by Bob Fryling, followed by a rousing standing ovation. Never one known for being shy or for letting his stature get in the way of recognition, Sire (who was sitting in the middle of the fifteen hundred who were gathered) stood on a chair to acknowledge the applause. When midnight came on December 31, Sire was happier than most that the New Year and the official day of his retirement from InterVarsity had arrived. Nonetheless, he continued to write and to speak around the country and the world, much as he had beforehand.

A Decade of Change

One day in 1999 Andy Le Peau asked an undergraduate editorial intern to help him clean out some old editorial files. As he was sorting what would be saved and what would be pitched, he came across a copy of some correspondence from an editor dated 1989. He waved the thin, pink piece of paper in front of the intern and said, "I bet you don't know what this is." As she looked at it, puzzled, she said she didn't. "This," Andy informed her, "is a carbon copy."

"Oh," she brightened with a note of recognition, "I've heard of that."

In less than ten years, the digital revolution had transformed almost every aspect of how business was done at IVP, as it had elsewhere. Carbon copies created in a typewriter were no longer needed. Laser printers networked around the office to every employee's desktop computer made it easy to make a copy for the file. Traditional typesetting equipment had been replaced by a desktop publishing system. Camera-ready typeset pages were no longer sent to the printer; electronic files were. No more were covers designed on boards with art pasted down and covered with tissue paper on which colors were marked. Now they were created on computer terminals with sophisticated design software.

While the technology was new, the mentality of frugality was the same. Traditionally, in order to place covers of backlist books into catalogs, production coordinators Wynema Marlatte or Shirley Peska would take two days to pull copies of actual printed covers from the files, mark them for sizing and tag them before shipping them off to the printer, who scanned them. Andrew Craft proposed to Nancy Fox that IVP do its own scanning, but the vendors said the quality would suffer unless IVP purchased a multi-thousand-dollar piece of equipment, something Nancy was reluctant to do.

Andrew thought the vendors were simply afraid of losing business, and so he suggested an experiment to Nancy and Don Stephenson. He would bring in his $300 scanner from home and scan covers for the next edition

THE GRAY BOX

One of the most tedious tasks each six months was updating order forms and catalog backlists. Changes were collected over the months on memos and handwritten notes. These were consolidated on handwritten 4" x 6" index cards (one per title) kept in a gray metal box that sat on top of the editorial contract files. Advertisements, flyers, brochures, catalogs—all had to be compared to the final, authoritative source, "The Gray Box," for accuracy. One of Sally Sampson's first questions to Allen Knight on coming to IVP was "Doesn't this place have a database?"

Several years later the database became a reality. Don Stephenson had been frustrated that Ron Lanier and Dick Ecker didn't have enough time to run the reports Don wanted from the mainframe computer. So he hired Andy Shermer part time. Don later agreed to allow Andy to help Sally create a database for all active IVP titles, using an inexpensive program called Q&A. Not long afterward Reuben Arulanandam began (and Mark Gates later reworked) a much more full-orbed database based on Microsoft Access for both books and authors. In April 2002 it was made available throughout the office on the intranet under the name Isidore (the prolific seventh-century writer of a dictionary and encyclopedia who is the patron saint of computer users and the Internet).

of the monthly IVP Book Club digest. As a result, the digital photo images were already embedded in the files, saving hundreds of dollars. Don and Nancy were satisfied with the quality of the final print product, and so IVP bought its own scanner. During one year, IVP saved about $10,000 on the thirteen issues of the digest alone.

At the beginning of the decade, catalogs, order forms, ads and other promotional pieces were handled in an assembly-line fashion—copywriters produced the text and sent it to design who then sent it to typesetting who took it to proofreading. The process was overseen by Shirley Peska or another production coordinator. The effectiveness of this approach deteriorated as time was siphoned away from building the website and the number of marketing projects increased (as did the number of books each year). In the meantime, open positions in production were not filled. Technology allowed IVP to handle more production work inhouse at less cost, such as Andrew Craft's proposal for dealing with cover shots. But the changes also had unforeseen consequences.

By the end of the decade, marketing pieces were routinely late going to the printer. Tricia Koning (who now handled production coordination under the sales and marketing department), Andrew Craft and Sally Sampson (the webmaster) began talking in earnest about why the work was bottlenecked and how to alleviate the problem. Their solution was to form a creative services group where each member of the team could handle most of the steps and would therefore be assigned whole projects rather than just a stage of the process for each project. That way when a major project came through, one person could devote time to it for copywriting, designing and working with the printer while the others in the group could keep smaller projects moving.

The head of sales and marketing, Don Stephenson, was not immediately receptive to the idea. Also, given the health of IVP director Ken De Ruiter, it was a difficult time to contemplate or implement a major restructuring. Sally Sampson continued to have conversations about her dream of a communications group after Jeff Crosby arrived in early 1998, replacing Don. Jeff wasn't sure that a group of designers and copywriters belonged in sales and marketing or that he had the background to manage the group effectively, and he did not feel the need to have functions such as these directly under his control. An additional advantage, in his mind, was that if someone else could oversee the new creative services team, he could focus his energies more directly on sales and marketing than other supervisory efforts.

So in late 1998, about a year after Bob Fryling took the reins, the creative services group was officially formed. With Anne Gerth joining IVP as head of production, Bob Fryling and Jeff agreed that creative services should be put under her supervision. Sally Sampson was designated to lead the team consisting of Kristy Odelius and two new people hired in early 1999 by Sally—Rick Franklin and Rebecca Vorwerk (later Larson). After a period of adjustment working through new accountability structures, the results became encouraging as more promotional material was created on schedule than would have been possible previously.

In 1990 all correspondence was through the mail or via fax. Ten years later most came and went as e-mail. Once all book orders came in via phone, fax or mail. By the end of the 1998-1999 fiscal year, 28 percent arrived electronically from distributors, chains and other major customers. This increased efficiency by sidestepping order entry and allowing orders to go directly to the distribution center. While most promotion and publicity was print-based, thousands of people were now accessing information about books through IVP's own website and hundreds of other web-

TECHNOLOGY TRIALS

IVP's production manager from the seventies, Jock Binnie, had a saying: "Given all the things that can go wrong in printing, it's amazing the ink ever hits the page." Computers, of course, help one make mistakes a whole lot faster, and that was sometimes true for InterVarsity Press. It has experienced its share of mishaps—many with the assistance of technology.

Mysteriously, text generated by an electronic file that appears on a proof occasionally fails to appear on the page. The covers of the first printings of *Written on the Heart* and *Perfecting Ourselves to Death* somehow were printed without the author's names. On the assumption that the authors wouldn't be pleased, their names were overprinted on the covers. Similarly, half of the subtitle disappeared from the cover of Wendy Zoba's *Generation 2K: What Parents and Others Need to Know About the Millennials.*

Text has vanished from within books as well. A volume in Linda Shands's Seasons Remembered fiction series was printed without the critical last page, and the first half of the introduction to *Dictionary of the Presbyterian and Reformed Tradition* failed to make it into the first printing. All these (and others!) were corrected before the books were released, but it made everyone even more attentive than they already were.

sites. Once no one ordered books through the Internet, but by the end of the decade Amazon.com was one of IVP's top ten customers.

All of these changes allowed IVP to get more books out more quickly to more people than ever before. While the digital revolution made work faster, one thing it did not do was make work easier. In fact, many employees found themselves working harder than ever. You couldn't send a letter off and wait two or three weeks for a reply before you took the project up again, getting other work done in the meantime. No, an e-mail response could arrive in a matter of minutes and demand immediate attention! The pace of work increased.

The expectations of customers increased as well. Since they could get an answer in a few minutes, they wanted it. Since they could get their books shipped the same day, they wanted it. Since they were used to seeing higher-quality design and production work in the media, in the mail and in the classroom, they expected it from IVP too. All these factors drove IVP into higher levels of professionalism. The new office building gave IVP a more professional feel. But the leadership sought to maintain an office atmosphere where people mattered, where it was still common for employees at office meetings to rejoice over the birth of a new child, to grieve at the passing of a loved one, to offer prayer requests and to pray for one another.

Technology also made it more possible for employees to telecommute. After four years in Downers Grove, Dan Reid moved with his family to Seattle in 1990 to become IVP's first remote editor. This suited Dan's work well. His coworkers joked that they never saw Dan anyway: "He'll be in his office for a year or two at a time and only emerge long enough to throw out a thousand-page dictionary." Phone, fax and the mail kept him in touch well enough along with two or three visits a year to Chicago. When e-mail and the Internet arrived, they increased the ease of communication markedly.

Soon others followed his example. Associate editor Cindy Bunch spent five years near Kansas City before returning to Downers Grove in mid-2000. When Greg Vigne took on the sales and marketing role of IVP campus liaison in 1996, he stayed in Vermont. Joe Suter worked in academic sales from Florida in 1999 after two years in the office. Electronic publicity manager Krista Carnet became IVP's most transient telecommuter. After spending a year in Westmont, starting in 1999 her life as a military wife took her in turn to Florida, Alabama, Tennessee and Georgia. In 2003, associate editor Drew Blankman also joined the ranks of telecommuters, following his wife to southern California when she accepted the post of pastor at a Presbyterian church there.

There were limits, however, on how many employees could work off site. Such employees needed to be especially self-directed, and their work needed to be self-contained. If significant collaboration was necessary for

THE DECLINE OF BRITISH INFLUENCE

Theologian David Wells chronicled the changes of influence that British authors had on the InterVarsity Press publishing program. In 1994 he wrote:

> There can be no doubt that, along with Eerdmans Publishing Company, the InterVarsity Press played a major role in linking British and American evangelicalism during [the fifties and sixties]. Since InterVarsity Press began its production in America in 1946, a total of 27.5 percent of its titles have originated in Britain. This figure, however, hardly tells the whole story because the number of titles published gives no clue to their prominence in the marketplace, a matter that is addressed in Table 19.1.

Table 19.1 British authors published by InterVarsity Press

TOP TEN INTERVARSITY TITLES

Financial year	Number by British authors	Percentage of top ten sales by British authors
1950-51	7	67.3
1955-56	6	58.9
1960-61	3	63.3
1965-66	4	63.3
1970-71	2	13.4
1975-76	3	34.6
1980-81	3	32.5
1985-86	3	29.0
1990-91	1	12.0

> The figures show the extraordinary prominence that British books had during the first twenty years of the press's life but also the considerable decay in that influence subsequently. Not only have British books captured increasingly fewer sales among the Top Ten books in successive years, but the press has carried increasingly fewer British titles. Beginning with the financial year of 1970-71, and looking at five-year intervals after that, the percentage of British titles carried is as follows: 31.4, 20.4, 20.0, 14.5, and 15.8. The projection for 1991-92 is 4.9 percent. It is possible that other presses have replaced InterVarsity as the favored conduit for British thought, but my preliminary research suggests that this is not the case. The problem seems to lie in the diminished capacity of British evangelical thinking to export itself.

a job, it was not well suited to telecommuting. There needed to be enough people at the home office to keep the flow of work moving.

While IVP continued to reflect and be influenced by its British roots, in the nineties this was clearly less significant. The writings of J. I. Packer and John Stott had been and continued to be at the center of the impact of English authors on North America. IVP alone sold more than one and a half million books by Packer and over six million by Stott. But it was not until the works of Tom Wright began to gain prominence in the nineties that a significant new British voice exerted influence on the American evangelical scene among both academics and the general populace.

In the nineties the mix of books at IVP also changed radically. The burgeoning list of Bible study guides surpassed one hundred titles in number. The reference line became one of the most highly regarded in Christian publishing with the release of the New Testament dictionary series and the ACCS. Likewise the academic list grew from a trickle to one of the premier programs in the industry. IVP's tradition of cutting-edge books continued to influence church and society with titles on intelligent design and openness theology.

In the late eighties, a new trend began to emerge—the development of superstores, spearheaded especially by the Barnes & Noble and Borders bookstore chains, a trend that came into full flower in the nineties. The stores helped smaller publishers by devoting substantially greater shelf space to topics like religion than was possible at mall stores. As more and more megastores opened and those shelves had to be filled with product, IVP sales grew. These general trade outlets also carried a higher percentage of thoughtful books than many Christian bookstores—making a good fit for IVP.

Independent Christian stores reacted to this competition by trying harder to make their shops unique. They cut down even more on the space devoted to books and increased music and gifts, items the superstores did not carry. A handful of bestselling books and authors dominated the Christian marketplace in fiction and nonfiction more and more each year. Most other books struggled to find a place in CBA stores. While IVP's passion for thoughtful, culture-engaging books did not change, the appetite of Christian bookstores for such books did change. As a result, readers interested

CHRISTIAN BOOKSELLERS ASSOCIATION—CBA

The Christian Booksellers Association has gathered together Christian bookstore owners and operators for over five decades. It held its first convention September 13-16, 1950, at the Hotel LaSalle in Chicago, beginning with 219 charter member stores and setting up its offices at Moody Press. By 1961 it had grown to 830 stores, and in 1969 it moved its annual convention out of a hotel and to a convention center, meeting in Cincinnati. Two decades later, in 1989, attendance at the annual convention (also called CBA), surpassed ten thousand for the first time.

InterVarsity Press first displayed at the convention in the 1950s and was attending regularly in the late 1960s. It became the major annual event for selling and marketing IVP books. With a sales force of only one, two or three to visit thousands of stores in the 1960s and 1970s, IVP found the convention all the more important for connecting with stores face-to-face. Unlike its counterpart in the American Booksellers Association, the CBA convention was not so much a place to schmooze, network and promote. Rather, IVP (and dozens of other Christian publishers) wrote tens of thousands of dollars worth of orders during the four days of the convention, which was sometimes equal to nearly a month's worth of sales.

As the convention grew, it became more of a challenge to get the attention of store owners, who were also lured by purveyors of gifts and other religious goods that have higher margin for storeowners than books do. Music also began to grow into a huge industry, eroding even further the amount of space stores devoted to books. IVP sought to keep their interest with new deals on discount, billing and shipping. Key authors were brought to the convention to autograph books, and the booth itself was made as attractive as possible. Under the affable direction of Sales Manager Jim Connon, IVP won the Total Exhibitor Award at CBA twice, in 2001 and 2003, an accomplishment achieved by no other publisher. Marketing's Peter Mayer created promotional videos on key new IVP books that ran in the convention hotels—something no other publisher was doing—beginning in 2000.

Despite all these efforts, by the mid-1990s, sales to the CBA market plateaued. This was exacerbated by the practice of Family Christian Stores buying independent stores that previously purchased IVP product strongly. Because the mix of product for each store in the chain was determined by Family headquarters, IVP sales in those stores were often reduced by 90 percent.

Other publishers noticed the same trend, and the convention changed from being almost completely oriented toward retail sales to serving equally four additional purposes—international sales, publicity, international rights and author acquisitions. The director of sales and marketing met with distributors from Canada, New Zealand, Aus-

Beginning in the mid-1990s until 2004, IVP used this trade-show booth, with an open feel and strong landmark tower, to present its new books. This photo shows the booth as it looked at the 2002 CBA convention.

tralia, South Africa and elsewhere who bought IVP books for sale in their countries. Radio, television and print interviews were arranged by the IVP publicity team. The editorial department met with international publishers interested in publishing IVP books overseas and also met with many prospective authors who knew this was a good place to find editors from many publishers in one location.

In 2005, CBA changed the name of its summer convention to the International Christian Retail Show (ICRS). Part of the reason for this change was to reflect the reality that books were only a minority player in the industry. Music and gifts had actually dominated for some years.

in thoughtful books began visiting Christian stores less and superstores more. Christian stores didn't adopt the strategy of stocking an even wider selection of Christian books than superstores did, beating them at their own game. The result became a self-fulfilling prophecy. By focusing on the "typical reader," a married woman in her thirties or forties, many stores narrowed their clientele and their sales.

Another trend of the nineties among Christian stores was an emphasis on "Just in Time" inventory. The idea was to have fewer copies of each book in the store and to quickly replenish titles as they sold in order to stay in stock. The concept was good, but the implementation did not help the industry. Book inventories were reduced, and dollars were saved. But instead of investing the money saved in increasing the selection of titles and bringing even more customers into the store, stores invested the extra dollars in music and gifts or in simply helping the bottom line.

The result was to drive IVP (and other Christian publishers) to find other outlets for their books. The "infinite" shelf space of Internet bookstores like Amazon.com, launched in July 1995, and Christianbook.com (operated by Christian Book Distributors—CBD) proved to be just right for the need. It increased the accessibility of books for millions of readers who otherwise had trouble finding specialized books in stores. The development of the Internet and the growth of superstores were encouraging trends for smaller publishers.

The nineties was a decade of steady growth, seeing the Press nearly doubling in size. Yet certainly leadership changes were some of the most dramatic of the period. Bob Fryling brought the steady leadership that was needed after a period of drift. He also enjoyed great credibility with the board and administration of IVCF, which helped give them confidence in the work of IVP. New department heads in production and in sales and marketing pushed new initiatives forward as well. These may not all have been the signs of a new millennium, but InterVarsity Press was headed there anyway.

Heart. Soul. Mind. Strength.

2000 and Beyond

≈ InterVarsity Press

> While postmodernity wants to celebrate diversity and other-
> ness, empires are all about hegemony and sameness. So
> while it is clear enough that the ineluctable forces of global-
> ization are indeed imperial in character, isn't postmodern
> disquiet something of a protest movement in the face of
> such globalization? Not necessarily.
>
> Brian J. Walsh and Sylvia C. Keesmaat,
> Colossians Remixed, 2004

The approach of the year 2000 was not exciting for those in the information services department at IVP. Concerns over Y2K (the computer
glitch in much old software that occurred because years were allowed only
two digits instead of four) had Ron Lanier, Reuben Arulanandam, Andy
Shermer and others at IVP working long and hard to remove any possibility of its creating problems for orders, accounts or other computer records.

Perhaps of greater concern was what effect it might have nationally or
worldwide. Some predicted that the nation's entire electric grid could shut
down, that bank accounts would go haywire and that no one would be

Thousands of Urbana 2000 delegates crowded onto the Armory floor at the University of Illinois, visiting mission agency booths (on the left) and the bookstore (on the right).

able to get any money out or buy anything. Some Christian books touted the tribulations Y2K would cause and how Christians could avoid trouble. All the hysteria, of course, was for nothing. All that happened was that a lot of people stayed home to avoid any potential difficulties.

Since people, out of fear, didn't travel much on that New Years, that made the decision to postpone the Urbana convention seem prescient. Originally planned for December 27-31, 1999, Urbana 99 was rescheduled to become Urbana 2000. The fear of Y2K (not Y2K itself), and the simple desire of many to usher in the year 2000 with friends and family, would have resulted in low attendance in 1999 and created significant financial difficulties. As it was, the Urbana New Year's Eve celebration at the *end* of 2000 marked the true beginning of the twenty-first century and the third millennium.

With Nancy Fox Scott's departure, Jim Hagen was assigned the job of leading IVP at Urbana 2000 and Urbana 03. Anne Gerth took on responsibility for the Armory sales team.

ETS, IBR, AAR/SBL

The so-called alphabet conferences of the Evangelical Theological Society (ETS), Institute for Biblical Research (IBR), American Academy of Religion (AAR) and Society of Biblical Literature (SBL), held annually each November, became the second most important conferences for IVP, behind only the CBA International convention each summer. These academic conferences gathered together thousands of professors of Bible, theology and religion, hundreds of whom assigned IVP books as texts. So as the IVP academic and reference lines grew through the 1990s and beyond, having a booth there became increasingly important to highlight new books and remind these academics of IVP's important backlist books.

The four conferences were split into two groups. ETS held its own conference just before AAR/SBL (usually in a nearby location), with IBR holding its meetings in conjunction with the latter. The booth for each event grew from one ten-foot booth space to two spaces, to three, and then to four and five. As sales grew, so did staffing, with sales and marketing bringing a half-dozen people or more.

The editorial department of IVP (along with those of other publishers) also used these events as prime opportunities for acquisitions or to work with authors on projects already in process. In the 1980s only Jim Hoover and Jim Sire attended. (While Sire went to sessions and chatted with authors, Jim Hoover was left to staff the booth and handle all the sales by himself, as no one from sales or marketing attended at that time.) Soon Dan Reid joined in acquisition efforts. Later Rodney Clapp and Andy Le Peau were added to the team.

In 1994, when AAR/SBL was held at the Chicago Hilton and Towers, IVP sponsored its first major event, a reception that featured a presentation by German theologian Jürgen Moltmann with responses from several others. This was so well attended that other similar IVP receptions were planned to highlight important new releases. For example, in 2000 Tom Wright drew a crowd when he was interviewed by Dan Reid, especially focusing on *Jesus and the Restoration of Israel,* a volume edited by Carey Newman that assessed Wright's *Jesus and the Victory of God.*

IVP had tried to promote the Book of the Day at Urbana 2000 through videos on the big screens at the Assembly Hall. But 2100 was overloaded with too many other Urbana duties, and these videos proved less than satisfactory. So at Urbana 03, with Greg Jao (former campus liaison for IVP and then IVCF divisional director in Chicago) as the master of ceremonies for the convention, IVP decided to go high touch and low tech. Greg, a voracious and infectious reader, was asked to give a brief announcement about each book—which he did with great enthusiasm. The personal credibility and rapport he gained with the eighteen thousand students, being in front of them for morning and evening plenary sessions, added to the effectiveness of this promotion.

A high-tech innovation for IVP at Urbana 03, headed up by Andy Shermer, Mark Gates and Andrew Craft, was the introduction of laptops and scanners at each cashier station. This system replaced the adding machines and cash boxes used previously. The networked laptops allowed for daily reports on how sales were going and, for the first time, gave an exact count on what books were sold at the special staff sale on the evening of December 31, making royalty calculations much more accurate.

The staff sale was a tradition that allowed staff to receive extra discounts on IVP and non-IVP books—so the book team would have fewer books to pack, ship and reshelve back in Westmont. The laptops had been tried at the staff sale at Urbana 2000 but the server crashed, and it was back to the old-fashioned method. But in 2003 it worked perfectly and the sale was done without long lines and in record time.

Electrifying

Technology can be a wonderful friend, but it can also create problems. One day Dan Reid got a very pointed e-mail message from a disgruntled professor who objected to the financial terms being offered for writing an article for one of the biblical dictionaries Dan was working on. He wanted Dan, among other things, to justify what he considered to be such a small fee for contributors by providing a detailed budget for the entire project. Dan knew it wouldn't be wise to respond immediately, so he decided to blow off a bit of steam first by forwarding the message to Andy Le Peau with a comment about how unbelievable and unreasonable this man's demands were. Immediately after he sent the message it occurred to him that he had not put in Andy's e-mail address. With horror he realized that he had not hit the "Forward" button but the "Reply" button instead!

The boom of the Internet in the late nineties had the publishing world abuzz and wondering where it all might lead. Would print become obsolete? CD-ROM encyclopedias like Microsoft's *Encarta* had virtually eliminated almost overnight the once-thriving print versions of encyclopedias. Was the rest of print publishing far behind? And if so, what platform would dominate? Publishers didn't want to back the electronic equivalent of eight-track tapes.

One company seeking to capture the electronic book market was Nuovo-Media, who promoted a hand-held electronic reading device a little larger than a paperback book that was called The Rocket eBook. NuovoMedia expected it to soon be as common as CD players. But they needed content, and in 1999 IVP became the first Christian publisher to sign up rights for several books. The device never caught on, however, and another attempt to market electronic books failed.

As the electronic surge of the nineties continued, Andy Le Peau met every year at CBA with a steady stream of software firms seeking to convince IVP to adopt their platform so it could create its own electronic products. Knowing how volatile the market was and uncertain which company would become most dominant, Andy adopted a strategy of licensing electronic rights nonexclusively to several firms rather than having IVP undertake the huge expense of publishing electronically itself. Another unsettled question was, What electronic product or products should IVP produce on its own—commentaries, dictionaries, academic books, some of these, all of these? What would be attractive to customers? It was difficult to know where to begin.

Eventually it became clear that Logos Research Systems had the largest customer base of any company, was the most stable and had the most academic and reference products similar to IVP's list (having produced products for publishers such as Baker, Concordia, Fortress and many others). So IVP in the United States and in the United Kingdom partnered together with Logos in 2000 to introduce their first CD-ROM, *The Essential IVP Reference Collection.* Rather than including commentary series, they decided to focus on the dictionaries and one-volume commentaries. The thirteen books selected contained over ten million words, and the CD-ROM sold well (mostly through direct mail), encouraging IVP to develop more in this area.

This success fit nicely with Jeff Crosby's overall decision to expand the direct-mail marketing channel even further. While the IVP website had grown impressively as an information tool, sales through this channel were only about $25,000 in 1998. Sally Sampson (now Craft) had long been the in-house champion for the Web since its inception at IVP and had long touted its potential as a sales vehicle, but she had lacked support within sales and marketing. Jeff now had a vision for making the website into a major sales tool.

Working with consultant Steve Gibson, he began to develop *IVP ChurchLink.* Sally enthusiastically supported these efforts and spearheaded the related Web efforts, creating for the first time with others in

TAG LINES

How does a publisher sum up its goals and "essence" in a few words? IVP has used several slogans, or tag lines, to describe itself. In the late 1980s Allen Knight introduced the slogan, "For Those Who Take Their Christianity Seriously," seeking to appeal to the best in readers who want to grow in their commitment to Christ.

After Bob Fryling arrived, he felt it was time for something fresh. Much discussion and officewide brainstorming ensued. Sally Sampson Craft thought something like the Wesleyan quadrilateral ("Scripture. Tradition. Reason. Experience.") would be good. Dave Zimmerman then suggested "Heart. Soul. Mind. Strength." And so in 2000 it was adopted. Based on Luke 10:27, this phrase expressed how IVP sought to bring the whole person under the lordship of Christ—our emotions, our spiritual lives, our minds and our bodies—a core value of the IVP culture since its inception.

the information services department (especially Mark Gates and Andrew Craft along with Ron Lanier) an effective shopping cart system along with a parallel website devoted to *IVP ChurchLink.* The first issue of the full-color catalog was then sent to twenty-five thousand church leaders in September 2001. Of course the international events of that month (9/11) dramatically dampened the result. Nonetheless, it was encouraging enough to continue, and issues have been released since then twice a year. As a result, sales on the IVP website alone grew over 1600 percent between 1998, when Jeff first arrived, and 2004.

In 2001 Canadian Andrew Bronson was hired to become IVP's first Internet and special markets sales manager. In the late nineties dozens of websites had mushroomed who wanted to sell IVP books online, Amazon.com being the biggest. This growing market segment needed special attention. And as the number of Christian bookstores continued to decline, IVP also needed to expand its efforts in making organizational bulk sales to mission agencies, Christian colleges, churches and other parachurch organizations.

With the success of *The Essential IVP Reference Collection* CD-ROM, it became clear that an editor would be needed at least part time to shepherd these and similar electronic projects through the system. So Andy Le Peau appointed Drew Blankman to the role of associate editor of electronic publishing in 2001. Drew had come to IVP with two advanced degrees in 1996 to work in telemarketing, handling customer service calls about academic books. Within a year he had taken a role as an editorial assistant, later being promoted to assistant editor.

At the same time, the e-team was formed—a cross-departmental group representing sales and marketing (Andrew Bronson), editorial (Drew Blankman), production (Sally Sampson Craft, chair) and information services (Andrew Craft, Mark Gates and Tricia Koning). The e-team operated somewhat like the R&D wing of the IVP website, keeping tabs on trends, generating ideas and implementing electronic/Internet strategy. The department heads and others joined the e-team to create the e-commerce steering committee, gathering occasionally to consider broader strategic questions. The IVP website, e-books, CD-ROMs, electronic rights and more came under discussion. With the electronic world changing so fast, it was important to coordinate efforts.

In 2001 the e-team proposed that IVP should publish and for the first time distribute through the IVP website its own e-book. Following the events of September 11, 2001, interest in Islam spiked. So before the end of the year IVP released *Islam: A Christian Introduction* by Winfried Corduan, updated from a chapter in his *Neighboring Faiths*. For an e-book, this achieved bestseller status, quickly selling over a thousand copies.

The Creative Card

While Andy Le Peau was working with Steve Turner to produce his book *Imagine* on the arts and evangelicalism (which was released in 2001), Jeff Crosby offered to try to secure an endorsement for Turner's book from musician and composer Michael Card, whom he had known for some time. When Card sent in the endorsement in January 2001, he noted that he had been working on a dissertation on creativity, so the topics in Turner's manuscript were fresh on his mind. Jeff passed this news on to Andy, wondering if IVP should pursue working with Card to turn the dissertation into a book.

So in March 2001 Andy met for lunch in Nashville with Michael Card and his manager. Andy noted the books that IVP was doing in the area of the arts and creativity. Certainly of all the Christian musicians in the country, Michael's thoughtful and biblical approach would make an excellent fit with IVP. The discussion went well, except for the fact that throughout the lunch Michael got progressively sicker. Something in the meal just wasn't sitting well with him. So the conversation ended and Michael went home to bed.

Fortunately, the meal didn't sour Card on IVP, and he sent a proposal to Andy in early April. Two weeks later Andy responded on behalf of the publishing committee, which had enthusiastically responded to the book idea, and offered a contract. Soon negotiations were complete and plans were made for a study guide and an audio book to be released along with the book itself. Al Hsu was assigned as project editor and shepherded the manuscripts through the process.

Hsu asked Card if he was planning on doing a song based on the book or its central narrative of Jesus writing in the sand in John 8. Card said no, he hadn't been planning on it, but he took the suggestion to heart, went back to his studio and soon wrote the song "Scribbling in the Sand," which then became the title track of his 2002 live album CD. The song and other creative elements and interviews also appeared on IVP's audio book for *Scribbling in the Sand*. This and the book itself, which was released in hardback, were IVP's lead titles for the 2002 fall season.

For IVP's annual author dinner at that summer's CBA in Anaheim,

Michael led some devotional thoughts from the piano, punctuating them with some of his own compositions. His substantive, genuine, artistic and humble presentation impressed the over one hundred authors, guests and IVP employees present.

A year later IVP released Card's book *A Fragile Stone,* a look at the emotional life of the apostle Peter. Card released a companion music CD with songs focused on this same theme. IVP also released the book along with a study guide and audio book.

At the IVP booth singer, songwriter and author Michael Card signed copies of his book *Scribbling in the Sand* for bookstore owners and other book buyers who attended the 2002 CBA convention.

IVP's artistic center for many years had been Kathy Burrows, who was responsible for IVP's corporate look, catalogs and ads while also designing virtually all its covers and the interiors of all its books for more than three decades. When she decided to retire, she gave plenty of notice, letting Bob know in 2000 that she would like to retire in the middle of 2001. Everyone knew such a search could take many months. And it did. Bob delegated to Anne Gerth the task of finding a replacement.

After considering hundreds of resumés, following up dozens of names, reviewing many portfolios, requesting sample designs for potential IVP books from several candidates, and reviewing all this data with those in creative services and with the department heads, Bob and Anne finally offered the job to a candidate shortly after Labor Day 2001—somewhat later than Kathy's original timetable called for. The candidate said he was positive but wanted just a few more days to make a final decision. During that period, terrorists hijacked airplanes and crashed them into buildings in New York and Washington, D.C., on September 11. This was a shock to everyone in the country. It affected the design candidate so much that he decided to opt for the stability of his current job rather than make a switch just then.

Anne was back to square one and quite discouraged. Such was Kathy's loyalty to IVP, however, that she was willing to stay on another six months or more if needed. The department heads decided to give Anne and everyone a break and not pursue the search for a couple months. The day Anne cleaned up her search materials and put everything away, the phone rang. Cindy Kiple, who had been working as the creative director at Crossway Books, had heard about the position and wondered if it was still open. Anne told her IVP was taking a break from the search but would gladly look at her work if she wanted to send some samples. The minute she opened Cindy's portfolio, she could see that her search had come to an end. It was some time, however, before a decision was finalized. After some extended discussions, Cindy joined IVP in late spring 2002, and Kathy was able to move into her long-looked-for retirement, where she could finally pursue her own art fully.

That same spring IVP lost one of its most prolific authors. John White died on May 11, 2002, at the age of seventy-eight, after fighting a variety of maladies. John had written over twenty books for IVP, with two books seldom on the same topic. John saw his calling as being something of a prophet, and he led IVP into sometimes controversial arenas, such as with his denunciation of materialism in the church (*The Golden Cow*), his embrace as a practicing psychiatrist of prescription drug treatments for depression long before that was accepted by conservative Christians (*The Masks of Melancholy*), and his support of John Wimber's Vineyard church movement (*When the Spirit Comes with Power*).

John had been a person of spiritual strength and intensity throughout his life. The integrity of his character and commitment to his Lord were the same, regardless of whether he was having a private conversation or speaking before thousands. At his graveside, one of his sons recalled going on a walk with John shortly before his death. He asked his father, "Have you ever been upset with God about the Alzheimer's?" The response was a firm shake of the head back and forth. "You've never been upset about the Alzheimer's?" his son asked again. This time the head nodded.

John said, "Yes, upset about the Alzheimer's. Never mad at God." At this point, as they walked, John began to sing from memory:

All the way my Savior leads me;
What have I to ask beside?
Can I doubt His tender mercy,
Who through life has been my Guide?
Heav'nly peace, divinest comfort,
Here by faith in Him to dwell!
For I know whate'er befall me,
Jesus doeth all things well;
For I know whate'er befall me,
Jesus doeth all things well.

Those gathered at his funeral sang that hymn together, celebrating a life lived well and lived for God.

Not long afterward, IVP said a different sort of goodbye to two long-time IVP employees who both retired in 2003, Linda Doll and Dot Bowman. Dot Bowman had come in 1965, working as Jim Nyquist's administrative assistant and assistant to the editorial department. Later she single-handedly provided for IVP's word processing needs. She retired the first time in 1990 but came back a few years later, working on the IVP Book Club and continuity programs until her second retirement.

Visiting the Pope

Tom Oden, series editor of the Ancient Christian Commentary on Scripture, was granted an audience with his Holiness John Paul II on December 3, 2003, along with several of his key associates in developing the ACCS.

The audience was arranged by Città Nuova, IVP's ACCS publishing partner in Italy, who also accompanied the ACCS team for the audience. The occasion was the publication of the first volumes of the Italian edition of the ACCS, including the two volumes on Matthew and the volume Tom himself edited on Mark.

The Italian publisher saw this as such a significant publishing event for them and the church that they wanted to mark the occasion by presenting

On December 3, 2003, Pope John Paul II received copies of the Italian and Spanish editions of *Mark* (ACCS) from (l. to r.) Giovanni Battista Dadda (publisher of the Italian publishing house Città Nuova for the ACCS), Donato Falmi (editorial director, Città Nuova) and Thomas C. Oden (general editor of the ACCS).

the volumes to the pope. Prior to the audience, the ACCS team also met with a representative from the Pontifical Institute on Christian Unity in order to discuss the current ecumenical situation. There was also some discussion of the contribution the ACCS had made toward ecumenical dialogue through its ability to gather scholars from across denominational lines who, nonetheless, could appeal to a common source and tradition in the interpretation of Scripture.

Bolstering Sales

In the fall of 2003, sales across the Christian publishing industry began to take a double-digit fall, and IVP was affected along with most other publishers. One of the primary reasons was weakness in the Christian bookstore channel. Many strong independent stores had been purchased by Christian chains that focused on a limited stock of bestsellers. Competition from major chains like Borders and Barnes & Noble, as well as from the Internet and mass merchandisers like Wal-Mart, was also having a major impact.

Recognizing these trends long before, IVP had made some moves to expand into other markets. But now even more significant action was needed. So that fall Jeff Crosby switched sales representation from the Consortium Group (which IVP had used since 1990, before which IVP had its own full-time traveling sales reps) to Noble Marketing. This move increased the number of stores being reached personally with IVP books from about 600 to about 1,400 independent Christian stores, trade stores and academic stores.

The next year Crosby also signed up Midpoint Trade Books to represent IVP to the major chains such as Borders, Barnes & Noble, and Books-A-Million. Sales through Amazon.com (which didn't exist in 1994) also grew strongly, making Amazon IVP's number two customer in 2006, just behind distribution giant Ingram/Spring Arbor. New time and energy focused on Family Christian Stores and on Ingram/Spring Arbor also had a significant impact on sales. As a result of those efforts, good sales at Urbana 03 and a new bestseller, IVP not only overcame its sales deficit but had a record year.

What was the bestseller? IVP published its first *New York Times* Bestseller in 2004 when *Finding God in the Questions* by Dr. Timothy Johnson of ABC News made the top ten list for "Hardcover Advice" books. The book's journey to IVP began when Johnson met Mary Anne Phemister and her husband, Bill, at a conference where Bill was playing the piano and Tim was one of the speakers. In April 2001 he mentioned to Mary Anne that he was writing a book and asked if she would read his draft copy and give him some feedback. She was glad to do so but thought that Bob Fryling, who was in her covenant group at First Presbyterian Church of Glen Ellyn, Illinois, might be a better person to do so (Mary Anne and Bill had been part of InterVarsity in New York in their student days). With Johnson's consent she gave the manuscript to Bob, and he read it the next evening. Bob thought it had possibilities but also thought it would need some theological input.

Bob made copies for Andy and Jeff, who agreed it wasn't right for IVP in its current form. But Bob hated to just say no. So he called Tim the next day and talked with him about Tim's passion for the book as well as the pros and cons of publishing with an evangelical publisher like IVP versus a more general publisher like Doubleday. Tim's desire to reach those on the edge of faith was something IVP certainly believed in. Johnson wanted to gain a reading from those who had been turned off by the institutional church, who feared religious "fanatics," and present them with a reasonable perspective on faith and with an inviting portrait of Jesus.

On April 12 Bob wrote to Tim with some suggestions for the manuscript and a copy of IVP's Purpose and Values Statement (see appendix 4) so that he would know more fully who IVP was as a publisher. Bob said IVP would be very willing to seriously consider a manuscript revised in light of the various issues he had raised. If not, Bob wished him well in finding another publisher.

One week later Tim agreed to revise the book, and he sent his new version to Bob in June 2001. Questions still remained, however, which Bob detailed in a three-page letter. He commended the work of N. T. Wright on Jesus and the New Testament, pointing out that the Jesus Seminar was not in the center of biblical scholarship even in mainline circles. Likewise, given Tim's interests in science, Bob introduced him to the work of Phillip Johnson and others in the intelligent design movement. Once again Bob mentioned the possibility of Tim's pursuing a general trade publisher and honestly thought that would be the route Tim would take.

Bob was therefore surprised, in the fall of that year, when Tim called to say that he and his wife, Nancy, were passing through Chicago and asked if they could have dinner with Bob and his wife, Alice. This and several other meals together were an important part of the process of building a solid relationship.

As a result, Tim sent yet another major revision of the manuscript. It was clear that despite repeatedly mentioning that a nonreligious publisher might be better for him, Johnson was serious about working with IVP. Andy Le Peau, Jim Hoover and Al Hsu then wrote in-depth reports. These were sent to Tim, who then visited IVP in the spring of 2002 to work through the issues one by one with the editors.

After more careful work by Tim, contractual negotiations were completed and plans for the release of *Finding God in the Questions* began in earnest, including the production (for only the second time in IVP's history) of seven hundred advance reader copies of the book—a paperback version sent to magazines, newspapers and book buyers. It was the first time in IVP's history that a book was launched with a "street date." Thousands of copies were sent to those who had pre-ordered, with instructions not to make it available for sale to retail customers before May 18. This helped to signal the importance of the book, created some buzz and gave each retailer an equal chance to sell the book to its constituency.

On May 18 a dessert reception for family and friends of Tim as well as alumni and donors of IVCF was held outside Boston (Tim's home town) at Christian Book Distributors' offices. Tim signed copies of his book both before and after Bob interviewed him about the book.

Following a book signing at the American Bible Society Bookstore at 1865 Broadway in New York on May 26, a dinner reception was held at Le Parker Meridian Hotel. After the meal Bob introduced Tim, the book and its significance. Tim responded with appreciation and then, as had been agreed ahead of time, invited Peter Jennings to interview him about the book. Rather than stand behind a podium, they sat on the sill of the huge windows overlooking Central Park. Those present were captivated by these two thoughtful, bright communicators wrestling with eternal spiritual issues as friends and colleagues who had different convictions, discussing some of the key questions of the book such as undeserved suffering in the world and the uniqueness of Jesus.

Jennings even admitted that he had tried to talk Tim out of publishing the book. He was concerned that it would damage his friend's reputation, that Tim would be viewed as some kind of "religious nut." But while riding in a limo he had read in that morning's *Wall Street Journal* a review of the book, and the reviewer had clearly understood and appreciated what

OPENNESS AND ETS

IVP found itself at the center of controversy at the Evangelical Theological Society meetings in 2001. Discussion had been growing since IVP published *The Openness of God* in 1994, the first book proposing what came to be called "openness theology." The theme at the Colorado Springs ETS conference that year was "Defining Evangelicalism's Boundaries," and there was a huge run on several new IVP books on the topic of openness theology—*God and Time, Divine Foreknowledge* and *Satan and the Problem of Evil.* At those meetings members of the society affirmed that they held to God's complete foreknowledge with 253 votes out of 360 cast (a position in strong contrast to that of openness theologians). While the vote did not change the Society's statement of faith, it clearly signaled what the majority thought.

At the next ETS annual meeting held in Toronto on November 21, 2002, Roger Nicole presented charges against fellow ETS members Clark Pinnock and John Sanders, arguing that their writings on open theism were incompatible with the inerrancy provision of the ETS doctrinal basis. The focus of the charges against Sanders was centered around his 1998 IVP book *The God Who Risks.*

Many thousands of words were written to present and to respond to the charges. After face-to-face meetings between the ETS executive committee and Sanders and Pinnock, Pinnock agreed to a change in his book *Most Moved Mover* (Baker) that satisfied Roger Nicole and other members of the executive committee. A vote was then conducted in a special business session at the ETS annual meeting in Atlanta on the evening of November 19, 2003. In the cases of both Clark Pinnock and John Sanders, the charges were not sustained, and thus these two members remained in the Society. Most members did not agree with Pinnock and Sanders, but there wasn't the two-thirds majority needed to oust them from the Society.

Johnson was up to. Jennings told the group with a smile that he immediately called Tim on his cell phone and said, "I guess I was wrong to worry."

Others from IVP enjoyed themselves immensely that evening as well. Senior Publicity Manager Krista Carnet had an opportunity to talk extensively with the producer of ABC News, and Print Publicity Manager Brooke Nolen assisted Tim as he signed books for those present. Jeff Crosby was in baseball heaven, since at dinner he heard all kinds of inside stories by virtue of sitting next to the medical doctor and trainer for the New York Mets.

The morning after that dinner, Tim took part in the first of a two-part interview on *Good Morning America,* conducted by Charles Gibson and Diane Sawyer. Soon after that, the book reached number twelve on Amazon.com's bestseller list. Johnson then appeared on ABC's *The View, CNN's Anderson Cooper 360°* and the Fox Network's *Dayside with Linda Vester,* among other shows. In September Dr. Johnson was the topic of the cover story for *Guideposts,* the most widely read inspirational magazine in the country.

Another book that exploded out of the gates in mid-2004 was *The Gospel Code* by Ben Witherington, a response to the bestselling novel *The Da Vinci Code.* Jim Hoover asked Ben one Friday in January of that year if he could write such a book quickly. IVP would need forty to fifty thousand words by June 1. Ben (known as a rapid writer) e-mailed back that same day that he could write two hundred pages in a week. Indeed, the following Monday Ben e-mailed Hoover over half the book! Less than two weeks later, the full manuscript was complete and, rather than the manuscript being written by June, the book itself was published in June.

IVP also saw the need to expand beyond the traditional Bible study market, which had flattened out over the years. The Through the Year daily devotional series, released in June 2004, was the first such series IVP ever produced. The *Emerging Culture Curriculum Kit,* IVP's first multimedia curriculum, released in August, was the first of similar products and won ECPA's 2005 Gold Medallion Award in Christian Education.

Mr. Pearse Goes to Washington

In January 2005 Welshman Meic (pronounced Mike) Pearse, author of IVP's *Why the Rest Hates the West,* was invited to speak on the topic of his book by the Congressional Institute at their annual Congress of Tomorrow Retreat outside Washington, D.C., for Republican senators, members of the House, spouses and staffers. About seventy people attended his session.

On the Saturday night of the retreat, Yale's Lamin Sanneh and Meic each spoke for a few minutes and then fielded some questions about America's role in the world. It was vigorous discussion, though not at all

Meic Pearse (far left) visits with President George W. Bush in January 2005 at the Congress of Tomorrow Retreat outside Washington, D.C.

unfriendly, and there were some good one-on-one discussions afterward. Pearse wrote,

> I was particularly impressed by my table companions that night: two main Republican leaders in the Senate and their respective wives who are really super people. . . . Their unguarded comments, and the snatches of overheard conversation, show them as being [concerned, for example] about the technical difficulties of making sure the vast anti-AIDS campaign in Africa can be made to work.

He also enjoyed a brief conversation with President Bush when he came to give a speech at Friday's lunch. Rudy Giuliani spoke that evening.

Meic had a variety of casual conversations with other senators and members of the House. His impression was that Christianity was the consciously and sincerely held worldview of the large majority of those attending. Overall, he felt the effect of the encounters was good enough that those thirty-five free copies of his book that IVP gave him to hand out weren't wasted.

Recognizing Stott

As 2004 concluded and 2005 began, national recognition came in a variety of high-profile ways to the author who had perhaps defined IVP more than any other over the decades. In the November 30 issue of the *New York Times,* columnist and commentator David Brooks wrote a stunning op-ed piece on how and why John Stott was the person to listen to from the evangelical fold.

He commented, "Falwell and Pat Robertson are held up as spokesmen for evangelicals, which is ridiculous. Meanwhile people like John Stott, who are actually important, get ignored." He went on to say what it is like to encounter Stott's books (no doubt many from IVP).

While John Stott had been a major figure in evangelicalism in particular and Christianity more broadly throughout his six-decade career, recognition from outside of the church came late in his career.

When you read Stott, you encounter first a tone of voice. Tom Wolfe once noticed that at a certain moment all airline pilots came to speak like Chuck Yeager. The parallel is inexact, but over the years I've heard hundreds of evangelicals who sound like Stott.

It is a voice that is friendly, courteous and natural. It is humble and self-critical, but also confident, joyful and optimistic. Stott's mission is to pierce through all the encrustations and share direct contact with Jesus. Stott says that the central message of the gospel is not the teachings of Jesus, but Jesus himself, the human/divine figure. He is always bringing people back to the concrete reality of Jesus' life and sacrifice.

Shortly afterward, the February 7, 2005, cover story of *Time* magazine, "The 25 Most Influential Evangelicals in America" also highlighted Stott.

He was called quite justifiably "one of the most respected and beloved figures among believers in the U.S. . . . He plunges the rich royalties from his more than 40 unassumingly brilliant books into a fund to educate pastors in the developing word [sic]." (Of course, there is a significant theological difference between the developing *word* and the developing *world*. While *Time* isn't always known for its theological astuteness, we add *sic* under the assumption that in this case the usage was inadvertent.)

Only two months later in a special issue featuring "The Time 100," *Time* numbered Stott among the one hundred most influential people in the world. The piece on Stott, written by Billy Graham, noted their friendship that began

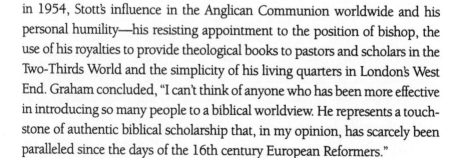

TIME'S OTHER INFLUENTIAL IVP AUTHORS

Besides John Stott, three other IVP authors were highlighted in the February 7, 2005, *Time* article on the most influential evangelicals in America. J. I. Packer was able to add to his many titles the honorific appellation of "Theological Traffic Cop." *Time* noted that the diverse evangelical "movement has no formal arbiter. Nonetheless, J. I. Packer, 78, an Oxford-trained theologian, claimed the role informally with his 1973 book *Knowing God*, which outlined a conservative Christian theology deeper and more embracing than many Americans had encountered."

Mark Noll, author of IVP's *The Rise of Evangelicalism* and many other significant books on Christian history, was highlighted not only for the excellence of his scholarship but also for spurring a renaissance of evangelical intellectual endeavors among others. The work of Bill Hybels, author of nine IVP titles, at Willow Creek Community Church was noted for his wide influence in training over 100,000 pastors each year.

in 1954, Stott's influence in the Anglican Communion worldwide and his personal humility—his resisting appointment to the position of bishop, the use of his royalties to provide theological books to pastors and scholars in the Two-Thirds World and the simplicity of his living quarters in London's West End. Graham concluded, "I can't think of anyone who has been more effective in introducing so many people to a biblical worldview. He represents a touchstone of authentic biblical scholarship that, in my opinion, has scarcely been paralleled since the days of the 16th century European Reformers."

At the end of 2005 it was announced in the Queen's New Year "honours" that Stott was awarded a CBE (Commander of the British Empire) "for services to Christian scholarship and the Christian world." (There are five classes of recognition with knighthood being the highest and CBE being in the middle.) Typically Stott, he was somewhat embarrassed by the continuing reference to the British Empire, which long ago ceased to exist.

Recognition of this sort from the wider world came late in Stott's career. In an era when so many Christians were known in the media for their scandalous behavior or extreme statements, it was refreshing to see one so solid and stable, one of such quality and character be given such well-placed public notice.

Discovering Judith Brown

Another IVP author received a different sort of national recognition about the same time. On April 7, 2005, Justin Taylor e-mailed IVP that he intended to run a column on his blog about IVP author Judith L. Brown, who had been sentenced to prison for the attempted murder of the husband of her lesbian lover. Taylor told IVP that the crime had been committed a year before the publication of *Discovering Biblical Equality,* to which Brown had contributed "God, Gender and Biblical Metaphor," one of twenty-nine chapters in the book. He had a series of questions for IVP and said he intended to run his column by the end of the day whether he heard back from IVP or not.

Everyone at IVP was completely surprised by this allegation. Andy Le Peau immediately called the volume editors, Ron Pierce and Rebecca Groothuis, to see if they knew anything about this. Andy's phone call was the first they had heard. They wondered along with him if this was a case of mistaken identity—that some other Judith Brown had committed these crimes, not the one who wrote for IVP.

Blogs (Web logs) had taken on new importance in the media, especially during the 2004 presidential election campaign between George Bush and John Kerry, driving issues and making news rather than merely reporting the news or offering opinions on the news. In light of this, Bob Fryling and Andy recognized the need to respond immediately, clearly and straightforwardly in order to keep the issue from snowballing.

That was all the more the case with *Discovering Biblical Equality* because it dealt with a topic controversial among evangelicals. The book was written by egalitarians who affirmed the differences of men and women without requiring hierarchy in relationships or the church. The blogger, Justin Taylor, was director for theological support in Desiring God, an organization headed by John Piper, one of the vocal leaders of complementarians, supporters of more traditional roles for men and women.

During that day and the next Andy was able to confirm that the Judy Brown who contributed to IVP's book was the same one sentenced to prison on March 26, 2004, six months before the book was published. He verified that Brown had started a church in Michigan, earned a Ph.D., developed Sunday school curricula for the Assemblies of God (USA) headquarters and been on the faculty of Central Bible College. She had met the Ted and Toby Smart family from Roanoke, Virginia, and moved into the Smart house temporarily and then next door. After a physical relationship began between Brown and Toby, on August 25, 2003, Brown entered the Smart basement and shut off the electricity. When Ted went down there to see why the power to the house had gone out, Brown struck him three times with a crowbar. He managed to wrestle it away from her and then called the police. Brown said she had no memory of the crime.

According to court testimony,

> neurologist Timothy Hormel said Brown might have suffered transient global amnesia, which can occur when an erratic heartbeat causes insufficient blood flow to the portion of the brain that controls memory. Forensics psychologist Evan Nelson testified that he diagnosed Brown with obsessive-compulsive personality disorder after her arrest and said she shows almost all symptoms of dissociative disorder. The presence of those disorders could explain why Brown reached a point in her life where she became obsessive and why she has trouble remembering the crime.

On January 28, 2004, Brown entered two Alford pleas, which meant that she admitted no guilt but acknowledged that there was likely enough evidence to prove the charges against her. On March 26, 2004, Brown was sentenced to thirty years' imprisonment, with all but eight years suspended. The IVP contributor agreement for Brown's article was signed by her on April 10, 2004. When she returned it to IVP, she gave no indication that she was in jail at the time.

Fryling, Crosby and Le Peau met early on April 8, 2005, and decided to cease distribution of the book and publish a new edition without Dr. Brown's article as soon as possible. A statement released by IVP quoted Fryling as saying, "This is a tragic situation for Dr. Brown, her victim and the many people associated with them. Although God does forgive and even use the writings of confessed murderers and adulterers like King David, the Bible also has clear moral guidelines for Christians who shepherd others." Three months later, in July, the new edition of *Discovering Biblical Equality* was published, with an article by R. K. McGregor Wright substituting for the one written by Judith Brown. There was no further significant media attention given to this episode, and the decision to act quickly and decisively prevented further negative publicity from gaining momentum.

Expanding Reference

The success of the Ancient Christian Commentary on Scripture led the entrepreneurial Tom Oden and Jim Hoover to develop related projects. In 2003 the five-volume Ancient Christian Doctrine Series (ACDS) was contracted, with publication of all five volumes projected for the end of the decade. Organized around the creed, each volume would include comment from the early church fathers on key doctrinal topics.

Two years later, in 2005, Oden and IVP agreed to produce at least ten volumes of whole commentaries by ancient Christian writers, all of which had been translated for the first time into English in the process of creating the ACCS. The Ancient Christian Texts Series (ACTS) was slated to follow the ACDS.

The most ambitious "spin-off" of the ACCS, however, was the Reformation Commentary on Scripture (RCS), an effort suggested by subscribers to the Ancient Christian Commentary on Scripture. The project would be of the same size and scope as the ACCS, selecting the insights on each passage of Scripture from the Reformers—something that, as with the ACCS, had not been attempted before.

Joel Scandrett, just completing his Ph.D. from Drew University, where he had worked under Oden as Translations Projects Director for the ACCS, was hired by IVP in 2004 to take the RCS under his editorial wing. The next year Timothy George, dean of Beeson Divinity School, at IVP's invitation, agreed to take on the role of general editor, with Scott Manetsch of Trinity Evangelical Divinity School as associate general editor. In Philadelphia at the November 2005 meetings of the AAR/SBL, the RCS advisory board met for the first time, with several members agreeing to edit key volumes. The target date for release of the first books in the series was set for 2009.

One key side benefit of Joel's coming on board was that Dan Reid could now take a well-earned sabbatical in 2006. After twenty years of editorial heavy lifting in reference book work, with many late nights and early mornings from his base in Washington state, Dan took the time for physical renewal in serious hiking and sailing as well as time at the Tyndale House study center in Cambridge, England.

A further strengthening of IVP's reference program came during Dan's sabbatical. IVP-UK decided that it was time to bring together in one U.S. publisher its Tyndale New Testament Commentaries (which had been published in the U.S. by Eerdmans since the early fifties) and its Tyndale Old Testament Commentaries (which IVP-US had published since the sixties). IVP-US had originally declined the New Testament series because its publishing program was just too small in those early days to take on the large project. By the time the Old Testament series began to emerge from England ten years later, IVP-US was in a better position to publish it successfully.

IVP-UK was looking to bring the two series together in a common trim size and cover design to make production and transfer of stock across the Atlantic more economical. They were also looking ahead to the day when CD-ROMs of both series could be offered to the public. IVP-US had already partnered with them on electronic product, and IVP-UK continued to see IVP-US as a strong partner in reference, as they had when IVP-UK moved the *New Bible Dictionary* and *New Bible Commentary* to IVP-US in the nineties. Therefore, IVP-UK made the decision to move the New Testament series from Eerdmans to IVP-US. The official transfer was set for January 1, 2007.

Brand Anew

As Jeff Crosby's tenure with IVP continued, he and his team began to notice a pattern that was inhibiting their ability to maximize their sales and marketing efforts. As they met and talked with customers, authors and readers, they came to realize that the breadth and volume of what IVP published created some confusion. Some thought IVP only produced high-level academic works while others thought IVP aimed primarily at basic introductory books for new or not-yet Christians. Of course, it did both. The accumulation of academic, reference, Bible study and general titles over the years had reached a turning point. The time seemed right for a new way of defining and explaining who IVP is and what it does.

Fryling agreed. In 2004 he embarked IVP (including sales, marketing, editorial, design, production and creative services) upon an ambitious two-year process of review and development of a brand strategy. Design and the creative services group, under the leadership of Cindy Kiple and Sally Sampson Craft, were given the task of developing visual expression for the results. On January 2, 2006, IVP officially announced it would divide its entire program and launch three new imprints, each with its own logo and tag line.

IVP Academic ("Evangelically Rooted. Critically Engaged.") incorporated reference books and academic books appropriate for the university setting. The aim of the imprint would be to provide the global university community with the very best of evangelical scholarship through books that start, shape, synthesize and summarize academic dialogue.

In addition, IVP Connect ("Exploring Faith. Shaping Lives.") segmented the part of IVP publishing that emphasized small groups, Bible study and curriculum. LifeGuides would be the flagship of the imprint with many other titles joining the armada.

Finally, IVP Books ("Think Deep. Live Smart.") brought together those thoughtful and practical titles IVP published for the general reading public. It included a wide range of topics such as apologetics, evangelism, discipleship, multiethnicity, family, church and mission.

Several subimprints would also be included under IVP Books to provide certain emphases in the publishing program. First, Formatio ("Tradition.

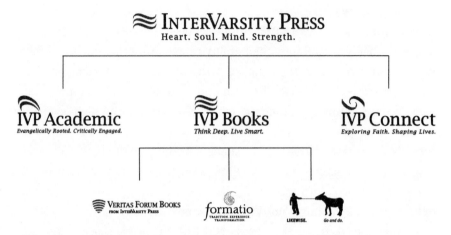

In January 2006 IVP announced that it was dividing its publishing program into three main imprints. Each centered on an area of emphasis that had been developed in previous decades.

Experience. Transformation.") incorporated the spiritual formation books from Gordon Smith, Dallas Willard, Ruth Haley Barton, David Benner and others. The line was formed because of the personal interest many Inter-Varsity staff had developed in classical forms of spirituality and the new openness evangelicalism was showing to Christian wisdom and practices from the distant past. Richard Foster had brought the classical spiritual disciplines to the attention of a wide evangelical audience with *Celebration of Discipline* in 1978. While the traditional evangelical emphases on Scripture and prayer were good, many evangelicals felt a spiritual thirst that was not being satisfied. The response to IVP books written by Eugene Peterson and Robert Mulholland in the eighties and nineties paved the way for this more deliberate publishing program.

Marketing and editorial also chose to develop practical, culturally savvy, globally aware books for twentysomethings (and those who think like them) that would fall under the name Likewise ("Go and Do."). Publishing for college students and those of a younger mindset had always been a central part of IVP's efforts. It was time to reclaim that heritage in a more intentional way. So books from Don Everts, Alex Gee, Karen Sloan and Scott Bessenecker were targeted for this line.

To help launch the line and get some momentum, IVP sponsored a three-day "Likewise Gathering" in June 2006, which was organized in-house by Dave Zimmerman and Andrew Bronson, and chaired by Don Everts and Margaret Feinberg (author of *Twentysomething*). About twenty authors and potential authors came to network, advise IVP, discuss their generation's needs, and examine how writing and publishing might be part of their ministry. The three-day event was modeled after previous consultations IVP had conducted for African Americans, Asian Americans and evangelical women in the academy.

The third subimprint IVP announced in January 2006 was a partnership with The Veritas Forum. In 1992 the first Veritas Forum was held at Harvard University, organized by Kelly Monroe Kullberg, followed by dozens more led by key Christian thinkers. The joint effort with IVP created Veritas Forum Books, which would discuss the tough questions of life and Christian faith. Kullberg wrote *Finding God Beyond Harvard*, which IVP published in mid-2006, the first book in the line of Veritas Forum Books. Soon thereafter, IVP obtained the rights to Kullberg's first book, *Finding God at Harvard*.

Strategic Partnerships

Joining with other likeminded organizations to create synergy for the publishing program was a deliberate component of IVP's corporate strategy in mid-decade. In a world of increasing competition for the attention of readers, doing so would allow much fuller access into important networks for IVP books and gain wider exposure for the partner as well. Thus IVP was on the lookout for such partnerships as the one developed with The Veritas Forum.

So Al Hsu was excited in September 2005 when he received a phone call from David Anderson, founder and president of the BridgeLeader Network and pastor of Bridgeway Community Church, a large and growing multicultural, nondenominational congregation based in Columbia, Maryland. David had been referred to Al by IVP author George Yancey. Would IVP be interested in discussing a multicultural publishing partnership? David thought he could bring a number of books to IVP by Bridgeway leaders and others in his networks that would help organizations foster multicultural effectiveness.

A series of conference calls between key BridgeLeader and IVP personnel discussing how such a joint effort might work culminated in a visit to Bridgeway Community Church by Bob Fryling, Jeff Crosby and Andy Le Peau. The three made the two-hour drive to Columbia one November Sunday from Philadelphia, where they were attending the AAR/SBL annual meetings. All three were impressed by the energy, creativity and sense of fun the church brought to its multicultural mission. The next month David Anderson and BridgeLeader's executive director, Angel Cartagena, returned the visit—they came to IVP's offices to work on both broad strategies and details of the overall arrangement. In January 2006 both the general agreement and a contract for a new book by Anderson was signed.

Discussion regarding another partnership also began in September 2005 with CAPS (the Christian Association for Psychological Studies), a professional organization of psychologists, counselors and professors. Because of Jeff Crosby's friendship with Mark McMinn (a longtime CAPS member), the two talked about whether or not there was a way the two organizations could work together. Jeff brought the idea to Andy Le Peau and academic editor Gary Deddo, who were quite open.

Jeff then arranged for CAPS leaders Paul Regan and Scott Titus, along with Mark McMinn, to join him and others from IVP for lunch to discuss a mutually beneficial arrangement of cobranding books with CAPS and IVP. The goal would be to identify, publish and together promote books that develop an understanding of the relationship between Christianity and the behavioral sciences. At CAPS's fiftieth anniversary conference, held in Cincinnati in March 2006, the two organizations announced they had signed just such an agreement. An earlier vision in the eighties for a line of People Helper books, which had failed to get off the ground, was thus fulfilled in this new partnership.

Other partnerships developed as well. IVP joined Zondervan and *Leadership Journal* in cosponsoring the 2006 National Pastors Convention in San Diego held February 22-25. Scott Bolinder, executive vice president and publisher at Zondervan, had often talked with Bob Fryling about various opportunities for the two publishing houses to work together. The convention had been held for several years with Zondervan

BEST CHRISTIAN WORKPLACES

Starting in 2003 *Christianity Today* magazine teamed up with Best Christian Work-places Institute and Christian Management Association to survey over 8,000 employ-ees in 150 organizations. They measured motivation, compensation, leadership, rela-tionships and professional growth, and other key categories that make an organization a great place to work. In 2003, 2004 and 2005 IVP participated in the survey and was recognized as one of the Best Christian Workplaces among small media firms.

as a sponsor. So when Scott suggested IVP join as a cosponsor, Bob took him up on the idea.

Here over fifteen hundred pastors from around the country gathered to lis-ten to key Christian leaders. As a cosponsor, IVP was able to arrange for many of its authors (emphasizing women and minority authors) to be part of the program, including Ruth Haley Barton, Brenda Salter McNeil, Ben Patterson, Rick Richardson, Efrem Smith and Sarah Sumner. IVP also gained sales expo-sure for its books and used the time to connect with other potential authors.

The very next month, IVP cosponsored the Serious Times Church and Culture Conference with Mecklenburg Community Church in Charlotte, North Carolina, the church pastored by James Emery White, author of *Se-rious Times.* White felt the message of his book was one of the most impor-tant he had to offer: These were life-changing times and it was paramount that the church know how to be salt and light to the culture. So he worked closely with Jeff Crosby to develop the conference. Several IVP authors led plenary sessions: Brian Godawa, Jim Sire, Kelly Monroe Kullberg and Michael Card.

The Way Forward

Bob Fryling often quoted an old saying, "The art of prophecy is very diffi-cult, especially with respect to the future," even as he set a goal of IVP dou-bling in sales between 2004 and 2014. The point of this first portion of IVP's strategic plan was not, however, growth for growth's sake. Rather, Jim Hagen knew that IVP, like any medium-sized business, needed to generate cash to fund its operations, and cash was normally generated by operating with a surplus. Growing too fast, however, could create great strains on cash (tied up in inventory or in waiting for customers to pay their bills). So a healthy but realistic target was set by the department heads so that IVP could continue to fulfill its vision.

Where would the growth come from in those years leading into the second decade of the century? The next part of the strategic plan addressed this question. As already noted, IVP planned to make strategic alliances with key organizations that could benefit both parties. Editorial would pursue regular publication of high-ticket items such as CD-ROMs, curriculum kits and large reference books. Marketing aimed to support these high-ticket items by expanding direct marketing through traditional mailings and use of the Web. It also looked to expand academic sales with deeper penetration into the hearts and minds of professors, sales to the general market through the major mass merchandisers, and greater emphasis on organizational sales.

To accommodate this growth Anne Gerth and Jim Hagen realized more square footage was needed for fulfillment. So under their leadership and as part of the plan, on August 18, 2006, IVP broke ground for a warehouse expansion. This not only doubled IVP's onsite storage capacity but gave the Press the opportunity to reconfigure the technology side of its order fulfillment system to meet the requirements of its largest customers. Upgrading the royalty system and integrating direct marketing programs with the rest of IVP's fulfillment software system were other key goals of the information services team for the rest of the decade. Last but not least in IVP's strategic plan was its aim to give all employees the training and resources needed to fulfill their job descriptions and the organization's goals.

As all plans change and are modified to meet new challenges and circumstances, IVP expected that to be the case with its plans as well. As Fryling regularly reminded the team at office meetings held every couple weeks, the spiritual component and IVP's reliance on God in seeking to fulfill its calling were foundational to its work.

Heart. Soul. Mind. Strength.

Writing the history of an organization that is still active and growing is something like writing a biography of someone who is in young adulthood or midlife. It is impossible to see the shape of the whole life of a person who may have many years ahead of him or her, and it is very difficult to have true perspective on how important certain events, decisions or periods may or may not be. Sometimes the effect of a book may not be seen for many years. Often a shift in direction that may seem critical at the time proves to be of little consequence in the long run. Only the perspective of years can aid in making reasonable judgments.

Yet certain themes have emerged in the life of IVP that continue to have their influence—a British evangelical heritage that is not afraid to engage the world of ideas; a financial frugality born out of years of operating a small, slowly growing business; a willingness to take calculated risks when they could aid the mission of the organization; the enjoyment employees have in each other, in their work together and in their fellowship with one another; the call to speak a prophetic word to the church and the world about justice and righteousness and mercy.

As this anecdotal history goes to press, the constant of change continues to affect IVP. IVP's ambition has not been to arrive at a penthouse in the media capital of the world or the halls of power in the capital of the strongest nation on earth. If that is where its mission leads, so be it. Rather InterVarsity Press has sought to remain steady in its continuing commitment to provide thoughtful books that encourage readers to believe, and to bring their whole lives under Christ's leadership—heart, soul, mind and strength.

Appendix 1

IVP's Gold Medallion Book Awards
(1982-2005)

The following Gold Medallion Book Awards were presented to InterVarsity Press from the Evangelical Christian Publishing Association. The name of the award was changed in 2006 to the Christian Book Award.

1982—Fiction
The Iron Sceptre
John White; illustrated by Elmar Bell

1982—World Missions
A World of Difference
Thom Hopler

1987—Christianity and Society
Crime and Its Victims
Daniel W. Van Ness

1988—Theology/Doctrine
The Cross of Christ
John R. W. Stott

1989—Theology/Doctrine
The Canon of Scripture
F. F. Bruce

1990—Missions/Evangelism
Disarming the Secular Gods
Peter C. Moore

1993—Reference/Text
Dictionary of Jesus and the Gospels
Joel B. Green, Scot McKnight and
I. Howard Marshall, eds.

1994—Reference Works
Dictionary of Paul and His Letters
Gerald Hawthorne, Ralph Martin and
Daniel G. Reid, eds.

1998—Reference Works/
Commentaries
*Dictionary of the Later New Testament
and Its Developments*
Ralph P. Martin and Peter H. Davids, eds.

2000—Theology/Doctrine
The Story of Christian Theology
Roger E. Olson

2001—Reference Works/
Commentaries
Dictionary of New Testament Background
Craig A. Evans and Stanley E. Porter,
eds.

2001—Christianity and Society
The Wedge of Truth
Phillip E. Johnson

2004—Reference Works/
Commentaries
Philosophical Foundations for a Christian Worldview
J. P. Moreland and William Lane Craig

2004—Theology/Doctrine
Old Testament Theology, Vol. 1
John Goldingay

2005—Christian Education
Emerging Culture Curriculum Kit
Jimmy Long

2005—Reference Works/
Commentaries
New Testament Theology
I. Howard Marshall

Appendix 2

IVP's Gold and Platinum Awards (1990-2004)

The following Gold and Platinum Awards were presented to InterVarsity Press from the Evangelical Christian Publishers Association.

1,000,000 sold
Quiet Time
Platinum Award presented October 1990

700,000 sold
Knowing God
J. I. Packer
Gold Award presented October 1990

510,000 sold
Basic Christianity
John Stott
Gold Award presented April 1992

5,243,000 sold
My Heart—Christ's Home
Robert Boyd Munger
Platinum Award presented April 1994

1,200,000 sold
Becoming a Christian
John R. W. Stott
Platinum Award presented November 1998

621,654 sold
Know Why You Believe
Paul Little
Gold Award presented November 1999

1,035,910 sold
Knowing God
J. I. Packer
Platinum Award presented November 2000

519,000 sold
Out of the Saltshaker and into the World
Rebecca Manley Pippert
Gold Award presented April 2001

505,378 sold
Too Busy Not to Pray
Bill Hybels
Gold Award presented April 2002

1,180,000 sold
Tyranny of the Urgent
Charles Hummel
Platinum Award presented November 2004

For a complete list of all of IVP's award-winning books, including those from *Christianity Today*, go to www.ivpress.com/info/awards.

Appendix 3

IVP's Multiethnic Publishing

The following books, listed in chronological order, are those dealing with multiethnic issues and other books by non-Anglo authors.

Three Kinds of Love
Masumi Toyotome
October 1968

Your God Is Too White
Columbus Salley and Ronald Behm
December 1970

Jesus the Radical
Ada Lum
August 1971

Jesus the Life Changer
Ada Lum
September 1971

How to Begin an Evangelistic Bible Study
Ada Lum
November 1971

Journey from the East
Paul M. Krishna
November 1971

Jesus, Zoroaster, Buddha, Socrates, Muhammad
Edwin Yamauchi
February 1973

Jesus the Disciple Maker
Ada Lum
May 1974

Single and Human
Ada Lum
April 1976

Independence for the Third World Church
Pius Wakatama
November 1976

World Mission
Ada Lum
November 1976

The Wind Is Howling
Ayako Miura
June 1977

Jewishness and Jesus
Daniel C. Juster
September 1977

The Impossible Community
Barbara Benjamin
September 1978

Pray Right! Live Right!
Bennie Goodwin
December 1979

The Effective Leader
Bennie Goodwin
May 1981

Jesus: One of Us
Brede Kristensen and Ada Lum, eds.
May 1981

A World of Difference
Thom Hopler
July 1981

Blacks and the White Jesus
Columbus Salley and Ronald Behm
October 1981

What Color Is Your God?
Columbus Salley and Ronald Behm
November 1981 (rev. ed. of *Your God Is Too White*)

Beyond Buddhism
J. Isamu Yamamoto
January 1982

Beyond Liberation
Carl F. Ellis
December 1983

A Hitchhiker's Guide to Missions
Ada Lum
November 1984

The Effective Teacher
Bennie Goodwin
February 1985

How to Be a Growing Christian
Bennie Goodwin
September 1986

The Urban Christian
Ray Bakke and Jim Hart
November 1987

The AIDS Crisis
Andrés Tapia
September 1988

Fundamentalistic Religion
(Global Issues Bible Studies)
Eva and Joshi Jayaprakash
August 1990

Multi-Ethnicity
(Global Issues Bible Studies)
Isaac Canales
August 1990

Sanctity of Life
(Global Issues Bible Studies)
E. Dawn Swaby-Ellis
August 1990

Urbanization
(Global Issues Bible Studies)
Glandion Carney
August 1990

Loving Justice (LBS)
Bob and Carol Hunter
December 1990

Luke (LBS)
Ada Lum
June 1992

Whatever Became of Fathering?
Michiaki Horie and Hildegard Horie
March 1993

More Than Equals
Spencer Perkins and Chris Rice
April 1993

Cross-Cultural Conflict
Duane H. Elmer
December 1993

Longing for God
Glandion Carney and William Long
December 1993

The Hispanic Challenge
Manuel Ortiz
December 1993

Penetrating Missions' Final Frontier
Tetsunao Yamamori
December 1993

Reaching the World Next Door
(rev. ed. of *A World of Difference*)
Thom Hopler and Marcia Hopler
December 1993

99 Reasons Why No One Knows When Christ Will Return
B. J. Oropeza
August 1994

Strange Virtues
Bernard T. Adeney-Risakotta
May 1995

Trusting God Again
Glandion Carney and William Long
June 1995

Haunted Marriage
Clark Barshinger, Lojan LaRowe and Andrés Tapia
November 1995

Free At Last?
Carl F. Ellis
December 1995 (rev. ed. of *Beyond Liberation*)

Black Man's Religion
Glenn Usry and Craig S. Keener
March 1996

Managing Chronic Pain
Siang-Yang Tan
August 1996

One New People
Manuel Ortiz
August 1996

Losing Face and Finding Grace
Tom Lin
December 1996

Ministry at the Margins
Cheryl J. Sanders
June 1997

Gods That Fail
Vinoth Ramachandra
July 1997

A Theology As Big As the City
Ray Bakke
July 1997

99 Answers to Questions About Angels,
Demons and Spiritual Warfare
B. J. Oropeza
August 1997

Defending Black Faith
Craig S. Keener and Glenn Usry
September 1997

Singles at the Crossroads
Albert Hsu
October 1997

The Gospel in Black and White
Dennis L. Okholm, ed.
December 1997

Following Jesus Without Dishonoring
Your Parents
Jeanette Yep, Peter Cha, Susan Cho
Van Riesen, Greg Jao and Paul
Tokunaga
March 1998

Spiritual Theology
Simon Chan
April 1998

Where the Nations Meet
Stephen A. Rhodes
May 1998

When the New Age Gets Old
Vishal K. Mangalwadi
August 1998

Beyond Family Values
Cameron Lee
September 1998

No Easy Walk
Harry Louis Williams II
November 1998

Faith on the Edge
Paul Tokunaga, Kevin Blue, Amy
Brooke, Robbie Castleman, Bobby
Gross and Jon Tran
November 1999

Diverse Worship
Pedrito U. Maynard-Reid
April 2000

More Than Equals, rev. ed.
Spencer Perkins and Chris Rice
April 2000

Faiths in Conflict
Vinoth Ramachandra
August 2000

Engaging Unbelief
Curtis Chang
October 2000

Urban Ministry
Manuel Ortiz and Harvie M. Conn
April 2001

If Jesus Loves Me, How Do I Know?
Christine Dallman and J. Isamu
Yamamoto
July 2001

Luke, rev. ed. (LBS)
Ada Lum
July 2001

The Scandal of Jesus
Vinoth Ramachandra
September 2001

King Came Preaching
Dr. Mervyn A. Warren
October 2001

Check All That Apply
Sundee Tucker Frazier
December 2001

Women's Liberation Jesus Style
Stephanie Bibb, ed.
December 2001

No Partiality
Douglas R. Sharp
January 2002

Daughters of Islam
Miriam Adeney
February 2002

The Prophet and the Messiah
Chawkat Moucarry
February 2002

A Beginner's Guide to Crossing Cultures
Patty Lane
May 2002

Chosen Vessels (Revised)
Rebecca Florence Osaigbovo
July 2002

Grieving a Suicide
Albert Hsu
July 2002

The Power of Friendship
Paul Tokunaga
July 2002

At the Beginning of Life
Edwin C. Hui
August 2002

Cross-Cultural Connections
Duane H. Elmer
August 2002

Changing for Good
Raymond Causey
September 2002

Thanksgiving
(New Studies in Biblical Theology)
David Pao
October 2002

Invitation to Lead
Paul Tokunaga
February 2003

The Sisters' Guide to In-Depth Bible Study, rev. ed.
Victoria L. Johnson
April 2003

From Every People and Nation
(New Studies in Biblical Theology)
J. Daniel Hays
July 2003

Kingdom of God (LBS)
Greg Jao
July 2003

The Message of Mission (BST)
Howard Peskett and Vinoth
Ramachandra
August 2003

One Body, One Spirit
George Yancey
August 2003

Get the Word Out
John Teter
September 2003

Secure in God's Embrace
Ken Fong
September 2003

Being Latino in Christ
Orlando Crespo
November 2003

The New Global Mission
(Christian Doctrine in Global
Perspective)
Samuel Escobar
November 2003

Jesus and the Hip-Hop Prophets
John Teter and Alex Gee
November 2003

Kingdom Come
Allen M. Wakabayashi
November 2003

How Sweet the Sound
Richard Allen Farmer
December 2003

It's Not About You—It's About God
Rebecca Florence Osaigbovo
December 2003

Unexpected Blessing
Cameron Lee
April 2004

God's Neighborhood
Scott Roley with James Isaac Elliott
May 2004

On the Jericho Road
J. Alfred Smith with Harry Louis
Williams II
May 2004

Raising Up Young Heroes
Efrem Smith
May 2004

Rise Up
Sylvia Rose
June 2004

Loving Justice, rev. ed. (LBS)
Bob Hunter and Carol Hunter
July 2004

Worship (LBS)
Sundee Frazier
July 2004

Being White
Paula Harris and Doug Schaupp
August 2004

Living in Color
Randy Woodley
September 2004

The Heart of Racial Justice
Brenda Salter McNeil and Rick
Richardson, foreword by John M.
Perkins
December 2004

The Human Condition
(Christian Doctrine in Global
Perspective)
Joe Kapolyo
March 2005

And She Lived Happily Ever After
Skip McDonald
April 2005

Growing Your Faith by Giving It Away
York Moore
July 2005

The Hip-Hop Church
Efrem Smith and Phil Jackson
December 2005

*Growing Healthy Asian American
Churches*
Peter Cha, Helen Lee and Steve Kang,
eds.
January 2006

Beyond Racial Gridlock
George Yancey
February 2006

Cross-Cultural Servanthood
Duane H. Elmer
March 2006

Subverting the Power of Prejudice
Sandra L. Barnes
March 2006

Hope for the World
(Christian Doctrine in Global
Perspective)
Roland Chia
May 2006

The Suburban Christian
Al Hsu
June 2006

Liturgical Theology
Simon Chan
July 2006

More Than Serving Tea
Nikki A. Toyama, Tracey Gee, Kathy
Khang, Christie Heller de Leon, Asifa
Dean and Jeanette Yep
November 2006

Practical Justice
Kevin Blue
November 2006

Reconciliation Blues
Edward Gilbreath
November 2006

Appendix 4

Purpose and Values of InterVarsity Press

In the mid-1980s, Linda Doll and the department heads developed a purpose statement for InterVarsity Press. A decade later, after Bob Fryling became publisher, he and the team slightly revised this purpose statement and added to it a values statement that was developed with input from all IVP employees. The following still serves as the guiding statement for InterVarsity Press.

Our Purpose

As an extension of InterVarsity Christian Fellowship/USA,
InterVarsity Press serves those in the university, the church and the world,
by publishing resources that equip and encourage people
to follow Jesus as Savior and Lord in all of life.

Our Values

Love for God, God's Word, God's People and God's Purposes in the World—Our identity is rooted in our affections and allegiance to God whom we seek to worship in spirit and in truth. We wholeheartedly affirm the authority and teachings of the Bible as foundational for our lives and for our publishing decisions. We love the church, respect and feed on its rich heritage and desire to serve it with grace and truth. We seek to influence, engage and shape the university world and our contemporary culture for the sake of Jesus Christ and his kingdom in the world.

Thoughtful Integration of Life—We value ideas and the careful expression of them. We love the life of the mind, of humble Christian scholarship, and encourage ourselves and others to "take captive every thought and make it obedient to Jesus Christ." We aim for integration of the whole person—our hearts tutored by truth, our minds shaped by godly affections, our bodies and souls surrendered with joy to God's good purposes.

Dignity of People and Relationships—We value all people as being created in the image of God. We celebrate the contribution of gender, ethnicity, church heritage and personality of each person. We practice a collegial approach to our work that entrusts others with meaningful opportunities and responsibilities. We value open and honest relationships. We care about authors, customers, students, campus staff, vendors and each other as people we can serve with joy, attentiveness, and trustworthy business transactions. We love to work and to have fun!

Beauty and Stewardship in Our Work—We value excellence, eloquence, creativity, skill and innovation. We desire to produce, package and distribute books and other resources in ways that reflect the glory of God. We like working in an environment that is clean and attractive and exhibits the beauty of God's peace. We also value financial integrity and faithful accounting of our business activities. We strive to be responsible and wise in using our resources of time, energy and money.

Notes

Chapter 1: Beginnings

page 19　　"There is a passion for Christ": Frank Houghton et al., *Quiet Time* (Downers Grove, Ill.: InterVarsity Press, 1945), p. 24. This quotation can also be found on page 25 of the 1967 edition, which is still in print.

page 21　　"the Inter-Varsity Fellowship of Evangelical Unions was officially formed": Oliver R. Barclay, *Whatever Happened to the Jesus Lane Lot?* (Leicester, U.K.: Inter-Varsity Press, 1977), pp. 9-10, 86-87.

page 21　　"Howard Guinness to travel to North America": Keith Hunt and Gladys Hunt, *For Christ and the University: The Story of InterVarsity Christian Fellowship of the U.S.A./1940-1990* (Downers Grove, Ill.: InterVarsity Press, 1991), p. 62.

page 21　　"requests for help from students in the United States": Ibid., p. 69.

page 22　　"HIS magazine was also created in 1941": Keith and Gladys Hunt explain how HIS got its name. "Robert Walker became the editor of the new periodical. Walker thought a one-word title for the magazine would be appropriate, after the style of the popular periodicals *LIFE* and *TIME*. Stacey suggested *HIS*, and subsequently found himself explaining to the Christian public that it was not presumptuous, that the magazine should be the Lord's and to his glory alone, and that all who read it should become His" (ibid., p. 94).

page 22　　"Gee, boys, I guess you sure oughta have a Q.T.": Douglas Johnson, correspondence to C. Stacey Woods on December 1, 1941.

page 23　　"IVP published its first inductive Bible study guide": Hunt and Hunt, *For Christ and the University*, pp. 96-98. The pamphlet does not bear the name "InterVarsity Press." Instead the cover reads, "An Inter-Varsity publication." While some printings of the work in the IVP archives give a copyright date of 1950, others list 1943. The IVP correspondence file for this title contains the Certificate of Copyright Registration from the Copyright Office of the United States of America, listing publication in the United States as December 24, 1943.

page 23　　"other Bible study guides were published": For example, *Look at Life with the Apostle Peter* by Jane Hollingsworth and Alice Reid was published in 1945, and *Search the Scriptures,* edited by Alan M. Stibbs, came from IVP-UK and was first published in one volume in 1949. *Basic Christianity* by Margaret Erb (1952) and *Discussions on the Life of Jesus Christ* (1956) also followed.

page 24   "Charles J. Miller took on responsibility for publications": Hunt and Hunt, *For Christ and the University,* p. 114.

page 24   Paul Hopkins "shared responsibility with Miller": Ibid., pp. 118, 424 n. 22.

page 25   "The publication of *Hymns* in 1947": Ibid., p. 109.

page 25   "Joe Bayly, who had joined campus staff in 1944": Ibid., pp. 110, 117.

page 25   "Although his way of meeting editorial deadlines": Ibid., p. 154.

page 26   "important as Eerdmans was in promoting": Mark Noll, *Between Faith and Criticism* (San Francisco: Harper & Row, 1986), p. 101.

page 26   Joe Bayly served on the board of trustees until 1982: Hunt and Hunt, *For Christ and the University,* p. 433.

page 26   "Joe wrote [the column] with grace": Russell T. Hitt, "Joseph Bayly: Tribute to a Prophet," *Eternity,* October 1986, pp. 30-31.

page 26   "When he 'wrote *The Gospel Blimp*' ": Ibid., p. 32.

page 27   "the decisive date in the revival of evangelical scholarship": I. Howard Marshall, "F. F. Bruce as a Biblical Scholar," *Journal of the Christian Brethren Research Fellowship* 22 (1971): 6, quoted in Noll, *Between Faith and Criticism,* p. 103.

page 27   "The first printing was 30,000 copies": Ronald Inchley, "The Inter-Varsity Press," in *Contending for the Faith,* by Douglas Johnson (Leicester, U.K.: Inter-Varsity Press, 1979), p. 323.

page 27   "staff members carried one suitcase full of literature": Hunt and Hunt, *For Christ and the University,* p. 115.

page 28   "To get the cash needed, Bayly sent out a letter": Joseph T. Bayly, letter to Mr. Roscoe G. Sappenfield, treasurer of IVCF, November 30, 1954.

page 29   "the British IVF has just about concluded": C. Stacey Woods, correspondence to Joe Bayly, May 29, 1958.

page 29   "a rocky road to Dublin": C. Stacey Woods, *The Growth of a Work of God: The Story of the Early Days of InterVarsity Christian Fellowship* (Downers Grove, Ill.: InterVarsity Press, 1978), p. 126.

page 30   "the first meeting of the literature committee": "Minutes of the First Meeting of the Literature Committee of the Inter-Varsity Christian Fellowship," January 9, 1959.

page 32   "Inter-Varsity brought into the American evangelical domain": Joel A. Carpenter, *Revive Us Again* (New York: Oxford University Pres, 1997), pp. 205-6.

page 32   "Christian students and faculty are a genuine part of the university community": C. Stacey Woods, *Growth of a Work of God,* p. 65. See also pp. 64-67. Similar sentiments were expressed by Woods in a 1945 HIS article on worldliness that was later published in 1949 as *Taboo,* one of IVP's first booklets.

Chapter 2: The Times They Were A-Changing

page 33   "Let us notice carefully that, in saying God is there": Francis A. Schaeffer, *The God Who Is There* (Downers Grove, Ill.: InterVarsity Press, 1968), pp. 145-46. This quotation can also be found on page 178 of the 1998 edition.

page 34   Urbana "takes its name from the location": The first "Urbana" was actually held in Toronto, Canada, in 1946. Two years later it was moved to the University of Illinois at Champaign/Urbana, where it was held about every three years through 2003. In 2006 the convention moved to St. Louis.

page 36   Richard Wolff was "a bright, aggressive man": Keith Hunt and Gladys Hunt, *For Christ and the University: The Story of InterVarsity Christian Fellowship of the U.S.A/1940-1990* (Downers Grove, Ill.: InterVarsity Press, 1991), pp. 228-30.

page 36   Nyquist's letter to board member Roy Horsey: Ibid., p. 231.

page 36   Nyquist asked to take on supervision of IVP: Ibid., p. 245.

page 38   IVP office moved to Downers Grove: Jim Nyquist moved to Downers Grove in the late fifties, following the lead of Stacey Woods, general secretary of IVCF, who moved there in the mid-fifties.

page 38   HIS editor Paul Fromer: Fromer, previously on campus staff in California, was HIS editor from 1960-1971.

page 43   "The name Inter-Varsity Press [then written with a hyphen]": James F. Nyquist, interview with the authors, n.d.

page 44   "Students were fighting to show films like *Bambi*: Michael Hamilton, "The Dissatisfaction of Francis Schaeffer," *Christianity Today* 41, no. 3 (1997): 26.

page 45   Wynema Marlatte (Paul's secretary): Wynema, a middle-aged woman, posted prominently above her typewriter in very large type the reminder, "HIS is not for old walruses."

page 45   "Eventually young people from all over the globe" visited Schaeffer: Colin Duriez, "Schaeffer, Francis August" in *Biographical Dictionary of Evangelicals*, ed. by Timothy Larsen (Downers Grove, Ill.: InterVarsity Press, 2003), pp. 583-84.

page 45   "*Escape from Reason* would have been published first": James W. Sire, foreword to *The God Who Is There: 30th Anniversary Edition*, by Francis A. Schaeffer (Downers Grove, Ill.: InterVarsity Press, 1998), pp. 13-14.

page 47   Gordon VanWylen and the first Logos Bookstore: Hunt and Hunt, *For Christ and the University*, p. 260.

Chapter 3: Expansion and Growth

page 54   "Christians and non-Christians have something in common": Rebecca Manley Pippert, *Out of the Saltshaker and into the World* (Downers Grove, Ill.: InterVarsity Press, 1979), p. 15.

page 54   Explo '72 on cover of *Life* magazine: *Life*, June 30, 1972.

page 54   "evangelical programs on television proliferated": Richard N. Ostling, "Evangelicalism," Believe Religious Information Source, http://mb-soft.com/believe/text/evangeli.htm.

page 55   "attendance at the CBA convention broke 5,000": "CBA Timeline: 1950-2000," CBA Online, <www.cbaonline.org/General/CBA_History.jsp>.

page 60   Urbana conventions were growing: Keith Hunt and Gladys Hunt, *For Christ and the University: The Story of InterVarsity Christian Fellowship of the U.S.A/ 1940-1990* (Downers Grove, Ill.: InterVarsity Press, 1991), p. 413.

page 61   "One evening [Schaeffer and Sire] sauntered": Scott R. Burson and Jerry L. Walls, *C. S. Lewis & Francis Schaeffer* (Downers Grove, Ill.: InterVarsity Press, 1998), pp. 109-110. Burson and Walls incorrectly give the date of 1973 for the CBA Convention in Cincinnati.

pages 65-66 "When the manuscript was done, I sent it to Jim Sire": Calvin Miller, "Preface to the 25th Anniversary Edition," in *The Singer* (Downers Grove, Ill.: InterVarsity Press, 2001).

page 66   "the most successful evangelical publication in this genre": Jan Blodgett, *Protestant Evangelical Literary Culture and Contemporary Society,* Contributions to the Study of Religion 51 (Westport, Conn.: Greenwood Press, 1997), p. 87.

page 68   Michael Hamilton on Schaeffer's influence: Michael Hamilton, "The Dissatisfaction of Francis Schaeffer," *Christianity Today* 41, no. 3 (1997): 22.

page 73   "HIS took issue with the former Miss America": Alvin L. Hoksbergen, "Is Anita Bryant Right?" *HIS,* February 1978, pp. 18-20.

page 74   "I'm sitting here reading a manuscript": Linda Doll, "Laughter," *HIS,* May 1978, p. 32.

page 76   "Jim Sire drew his first diagram of worldviews": James W. Sire, *The Universe Next Door* (Downers Grove, Ill.: InterVarsity Press, 1976), p. 9.

page 77   "The thinking of what might be called middle-brow American evangelicals": Mark Noll, "J. I. Packer and the Shaping of American Evangelicalism," in *Doing Theology for the People of God,* ed. Donald Lewis and Alister McGrath (Downers Grove, Ill.: InterVarsity Press, 1996), p. 192.

page 78   IVP as the primary U.S. publishing conduit for Packer and Stott: Ibid., p. 195.

page 78   Packer as an *"educated, Reformed, Anglican evangelical":* Ibid., p. 199. Author's emphasis.

page 78   The Lausanne Covenant: The Lausanne Covenant was produced by The International Congress on World Evangelization held in Lausanne, Switzerland, in 1974. The gathering was called by a committee headed by Rev. Billy Graham and drew more than 2,300 evangelical leaders from 150 countries.

page 78   Stott as the "sanest, clearest and most solidly biblical living writer": Mark Noll, in *Authentic Christianity,* ed. Timothy Dudley-Smith (Downers Grove, Ill.: InterVarsity Press, 1995), back cover.

Chapter 4: Years of Transition

page 79   "Stick-to-it-iveness": Eugene Peterson, *A Long Obedience in the Same Direction*
               (Downers Grove, Ill.: InterVarsity Press, 1980), p. 121. This quotation can
               also be found on page 125 of the 2000 edition.

page 83   Stott's Urbana addresses: John Stott, "Jesus Christ and the Authority of the
               Word of God," in *Jesus Christ: Lord of the Universe, Hope of the World,* ed. David
               M. Howard (Downers Grove, Ill.: InterVarsity Press, 1974), pp. 33-52; and
               "The Biblical Basis of Declaring God's Glory," in *Declare His Glory Among the
               Nations,* ed. David M. Howard (Downers Grove, Ill.: InterVarsity Press, 1977),
               pp. 29-91.

page 83   Tom Skinner's talk at Urbana 70: Tom Skinner, "The U.S. Racial Crisis and
               World Evangelism," in *Christ the Liberator,* by John R. W. Stott and others
               (Downers Grove, Ill.: InterVarsity Press, 1971), p. 209.

page 88   Sire's one Bible study guide during his tenure: James W. Sire, *Jeremiah, Meet
               the 20th Century* (Downers Grove, Ill.: InterVarsity Press, 1975).

page 90   Christian Action Council's review of *Brave New People:* "House Curbs Abortion
               Aid to China," *Action Line* 8, no. 4 (1984).

page 91   Letters of protest from people who had not read the book: James W. Sire,
               "Brave New Publishers: Should They Be Concerned?" in *Evangelicalism: Sur-
               viving Its Success,* ed. David A. Fraser (Princeton, N.J.: Princeton University
               Press, 1986), p. 140.

page 91   "Franky is in the midst of grief over his father's death": Joe Bayly, "Franky's
               Followers Call for Boycott of IVP Publications," *Christian Advertising Forum,*
               September-October 1984, p. 5. Bayly quotes from Franky Schaeffer, "An
               Open Letter to the Christian Booksellers Association and Christian Bookstore
               Owners and Buyers in America," 1984, circulated at the 1984 Christian Book-
               sellers Association convention.

page 91   Bayly further quoted Franky as saying: Ibid.

page 92   "By buckling under to political pressure": Richard H. Bube, "An Open Letter
               to Inter-Varsity Press About *Brave New People,*" *Journal of the American Scientific
               Affiliation,* n.d., n.p.

page 93   "The Schaeffers have disfigured their testimony against abortion": Richard
               Lovelace, "Extremism or Defense?" *Charisma,* November 1984, p. 9.

page 93   "Such are the tactics of those who fear the free contest of ideas": Steve Law-
               head, "What? Ban My Book?" *Christianity Today,* December 14, 1984, p. 76.

page 93   "a well-orchestrated campaign of demagoguery": Mark Noll, *The Scandal of the
               Evangelical Mind* (Grand Rapids: Eerdmans, 1994), p. 230.

page 93   "Eerdmans made an immediate decision to publish the book": Sire, "Brave
               New Publishers," p. 129.

page 93   "We couldn't shape up the others": Bayly, "Franky's Followers," p. 6.

page 94   "We must do our best to publish responsible books": Gordon MacDonald, personal correspondence with Linda Doll, July 25, 1985.

page 94   "I have read your article in the ASA Journal": Gordon MacDonald, correspondence with D. Gareth Jones, October 30, 1985. The Jones article MacDonald refers to is D. Gareth Jones, "The View from a Censored Corner," *Journal of the American Scientific Affiliation* 37, no. 3 (1985): 169-70.

pages 94-95   "Serious morale problems existed among some staff leaders": Keith Hunt and Gladys Hunt, *For Christ and the University: The Story of InterVarsity Christian Fellowship of the U.S.A/1940-1990* (Downers Grove, Ill.: InterVarsity Press, 1991), p. 331.

page 95   "Later both put their thoughts in writing": Ibid., p. 332.

page 96   "Since the president had ignored": Ibid.

Chapter 5: Years of Regrouping

page 98   "I could never myself believe in God, if it were not for the cross": John Stott, *The Cross of Christ* (Downers Grove, Ill.: InterVarsity Press, 1986), p. 335. This quotation can also be found on page 326 of the 2006 edition.

page 99   "James Sire of IVCF and IVP has influenced": Roger E. Olson, *The Westminster Handbook to Evangelical Theology* (Louisville, Ky.: Westminster John Knox, 2004), p. 82.

page 109   "IFES-linked publishing houses in thirty-three countries": "Publish and be blessed!" *Special Report: The IFES Magazine* 2, no. 5 (2005): 4.

page 113   "Rob Suggs's gift to humor": Calvin Miller, foreword to *It Came from Beneath the Pew* by Rob Suggs (Downers Grove, Ill.: InterVarsity Press, 1989), p. 6.

Chapter 6: Moving and Moving Ahead

page 114   "Stripped of all the theological debate": Spencer Perkins and Chris Rice, *More Than Equals* (Downers Grove, Ill.: InterVarsity Press, 1993), p. 57. This quotation can also be found on page 60 of the 2000 edition, which substitutes the word *criteria* for the word *actions.*

page 122   "Schaeffer was instrumental": Robert H. Krapohl and Charles H. Lippy, *The Evangelicals* (Westport, Conn.: Greenwood Press, 1999), p. 298.

page 123   "historians . . . would have to invent [Schaeffer]": James W. Sire, foreword to *The God Who Is There: 30th Anniversary Edition,* by Francis A. Schaeffer (Downers Grove, Ill.: InterVarsity Press, 1998), p. 15.

page 123   IVP's seminal or groundbreaking academic works: "A Message from the Editors: Our Rationale for IVP's Academic Line," *Academic Alert* 3, no. 2 (1994): 1.

page 123   Bloesch's seven-volume systematic theology: Bloesch had actually been involved with the InterVarsity chapter at the University of Chicago's Divinity School (see Roger E. Olson, *The Westminster Handbook to Evangelical Theology*

[Louisville, Ky.: Westminster John Knox, 2004], p. 52).

page 124   Phillip Johnson, Michael Behe and intelligent design: Josh Getlin, "The Case of Behe vs. Darwin," *Los Angeles Times,* November 5, 2005.

page 125   "Both sides ought to be properly taught": Peter Baker and Peter Slevin, "Bush Remarks On 'Intelligent Design' Theory Fuel Debate," *Washington Post,* August 3, 2005, p. A1.

pages 125-26 "God limits himself in relation to free human persons": Olson, *The Westminster Handbook to Evangelical Theology,* p. 326.

page 126   "Pinnock's 1986 essay caused some surprise and consternation": Ibid.

page 126   "I believe there was never a board meeting": Keith Hunt and Gladys Hunt, *For Christ and the University: The Story of InterVarsity Christian Fellowship of the U.S.A./1940-1990* (Downers Grove, Ill.: InterVarsity Press, 1991), p. 286.

page 126   "its policy of publishing thought-provoking literature": Ibid.

page 127   IVP-UK's publishing philosophy on controversial books: Ronald Inchley, publications secretary (that is, publisher) of IVP-UK from 1936 to 1977, wrote, "In 1946 we find the Literature Committee re-stating that 'the distinctive policy of IVP publishing should be to produce books concerned primarily with what the Bible teaches on the great major doctrines of the faith.' Two years later we find a special minute recorded, 'It was agreed that the Literature Committee should make it an overriding rule never to be committed to the publication of a book which does not satisfy the main requirements of our market, viz, fidelity to the Scriptures, scholarly accuracy, good English style, and strict relevance to the constituency which we serve, it being understood that it is better both for our imprint and for our constituency not to issue a book on any given subject unless it is plainly up to the required standard. . . . It was a policy discussion on whether or not IVF should tackle subjects on which Evangelicals were themselves divided which led to the suggestion during the war that an alternative neutral imprint might be adopted. . . . The idea received a general welcome and the name Tyndale Press was eventually chosen" ("The Inter-Varsity Press," in *Contending for the Faith,* by Douglas Johnson [Leicester, U.K.: Inter-Varsity Press, 1979], p. 321). Rather than being an imprint for subjects on which evangelicals disagreed, however, it became an academic imprint whose purpose was to work around the prejudice that establishment churches, schools or libraries might have against books with evangelical origins.

page 128   "Controversy over evangelical uses of postmodern philosophy": Ibid., p. 64.

page 138   "See how great a thing virtue is": Chrysostom, quoted in *Genesis 12—50,* Ancient Christian Commentary on Scripture: Old Testament 2, ed. Mark Sheridan (Downers Grove, Ill.: InterVarsity Press, 2002), p. 351.

page 141   "the most important project in religious publishing": John Wilson, "Bookshelf," *Books and Culture,* 4, no. 4 (July-August 1998).

page 144 "As the work expanded after the war": Inchley, quoted in *Contending for the Faith*, p. 321.

page 144 DeRuiter's CBA award: ECPO (Evangelical Christian Publishing Overseas) was the international outreach division of ECPA, which Ken participated in. ECPO later changed its name to Global Publishing Alliance.

Chapter 7: The Fryling Years Begin

page 146 "What Jesus did was not a mere example": N. T. Wright, *The Challenge of Jesus* (Downers Grove, Ill.: InterVarsity Press, 1999), p. 178.

pages 146-47 Fryling's work history with IVCF: Keith Hunt and Gladys Hunt, *For Christ and the University: The Story of InterVarsity Christian Fellowship of the U.S.A/1940-1990* (Downers Grove, Ill.: InterVarsity Press, 1991), p. 443.

page 153 "On January 2, 1999": N. T. Wright, *The Challenge of Jesus* (Downers Grove, Ill.: InterVarsity Press, 1999), p. 9.

page 160 "The Decline of British Influence": David Wells, "On Being Evangelical," in *Evangelicalism,* ed. Mark A. Noll, David Bebbington, and George A. Rawlyk (New York: Oxford, 1994), p. 395.

page 161 The prominence of Wright's books in the nineties: Wright's books have been published in the U.S. by HarperSanFrancisco, Eerdmans, Westminster John Knox, InterVarsity Press and others. His influence began to rise sharply with his multivolume Christian Origins and the Question of God, a series whose first volume was published in 1996 in the United Kingdom by SPCK and in the United States by Fortress Press. His "For Everyone" series on each book of the New Testament, published by Westminster John Knox, shows his range in also being able to reach a popular readership.

page 162 The growth of CBA: "CBA Timeline: 1950-2000," CBA Online <www.cbaonline.org/General/CBA_History.jsp>.

Chapter 8: Heart. Soul. Mind. Strength.

page 165 "While postmodernity wants to celebrate diversity and otherness": Brian J. Walsh and Sylvia C. Keesmaat, *Colossians Remixed* (Downers Grove, Ill.: InterVarsity Press, 2004), p. 31.

page 175 Fanny Crosby, "All the Way My Savior Leads Me," 1875.

page 179 *Wall Street Journal* review of Tim Johnson's book: Susan Lee, "The Physician Examines Faith," *Wall Street Journal,* May 26, 2004, p. D12.

page 180 "I guess I was wrong to worry": Timothy Johnson, *Finding God in the Questions,* 2nd ed. (Downers Grove, Ill.: InterVarsity Press, 2006), p. 202.

page 182 "I was particularly impressed by my table companions": Meic Pearse, "Back, Bemused, from the Heart of the GOP," unpublished article, 2005.

page 183 *New York Times* on John Stott: David Brooks, "Who Is John Stott?" *New York*

Times (late ed.), November 30, 2004, A23.

page 184   "One of the most respected": "The 25 Most Influential Evangelicals in America," *Time,* February 7, 2005, p. 45.

page 184   *Time* magazine on Packer: Ibid., p. 41.

page 184   *Time* magazine on Noll: Ibid., p. 42.

page 184   *Time* magazine on Hybels: Ibid., p. 45.

page 184   "I cannot think of anyone": Billy Graham, "Teacher of the Faith: John Stott" *Time,* April 18, 2005, p. 103.

page 185   Queen honors Stott with CBE: Daniel Blake, "Evangelical Rev John Stott Celebrated in Queen's New Year Honours List," *ChristianityToday,* January 5, 2005 <www.christiantoday.com/article/evangelical.rev.john.stott.celebrated .in.queens.new.year.honours.list/4935.htm>.

page 185   "Blogs (Web logs) had taken on new importance in the media": For example, blogs that were supportive of President Bush had also been instrumental in showing that evidence had been faked which CBS used to question George Bush's National Guard service, with the eventual dismissal of several CBS employees.

page 186   "Neurologist Timothy Hormel": Lindsey Nair, "Woman to Serve 8 Years for Attack on Minister," *Roanoke Times and World News,* March 27, 2004, p. A1.

pages 186-87 Brown's sentencing: Meg Hibbert, "Minister Sentenced to 30 Years," March 27, 2004, Mainstreetnewspapers.com <www.mainstreetnewspapers.com/articles/2004/04/05/salem/news/news01.txt>.

page 193   "The art of prophecy is very difficult": The saying is attributed both to the Chinese and to Mark Twain.

Bibliography

Archives of the Billy Graham Center, Wheaton, Illinois. Collection 300, Records of the Inter-Varsity Christian Fellowship.

Balmer, Randall. *Encyclopedia of Evangelicalism.* Waco, Tex.: Baylor University Press, 2004.

Barclay, Oliver R. *Whatever Happened to the Jesus Lane Lot?* Leicester, U.K.: InterVarsity Press, 1977.

"CBA Timeline: 1950-2000." CBA Online <www.cbaonline.org/General/CBA_History.jsp>.

"Civic Center, to Plumbing, to Garage, to Publishing," *Downers Grove Reporter,* June 30, 1982.

"Fifty Years of Front-Line Publishing." Inter-Varsity Press, England, 1986.

Grahmann, Bob. "The History of InterVarsity Press." InterVarsity Christian Fellowship <www.intervarsity.org/staff/library/ivp.html>. This piece is mistitled. It is actually a history of Bible study in IVCF, which includes some material on IVP.

HIS magazine and U magazine bound volumes. 1941-1988. InterVarsity Christian Fellowship/USA.

Hitt, Russell T. "Joseph Bayly: Tribute to a Prophet," *Eternity,* October 1986.

Hunt, Keith, and Gladys Hunt. *For Christ and the University.* Downers Grove, Ill.: InterVarsity Press. 1991.

InterVarsity Press correspondence files. InterVarsity Press, Westmont, Ill.

Johnson, Douglas. *Contending for the Faith: A History of the Evangelical Movement in the Universities and Colleges.* Leicester, U.K.: Inter-Varsity Press, 1979.

Larsen, Timothy, et al., eds. *Biographical Dictionary of Evangelicals.* Downers Grove, Ill.: InterVarsity Press, 2003.

Munger, Robert Boyd. "The Story of My Heart—Christ's Home." In *My Heart—Christ's Home: A Story for Old and Young.* Illustrated Adult Gift Edition. Downers Grove, Ill.: InterVarsity Press, 1992.

Noll, Mark. "J. I. Packer and the Shaping of American Evangelicalism." In *Doing Theology for the People of God.* Edited by Donald Lewis and Alister McGrath. Downers Grove, Ill.: InterVarsity Press, 1996.

Olson, Roger E. *The Westminster Handbook to Evangelical Theology.* Louisville, Ky.: Westminster John Knox Press, 2004.

Sire, James W. "Brave New Publishers: Should They Be Concerned?" In *Evangelicalism: Surviving Its Success.* Edited by David A. Fraser. Princeton, N.J.: Princeton University Press, 1986.

Sire, James W. Foreword to *The God Who Is There,* by Francis A. Schaeffer. Downers Grove, Ill.: InterVarsity Press, 1998.

Woods, C. Stacey. *The Growth of a Work of God: The Story of the Early Days of InterVarsity Christian Fellowship.* Downers Grove, Ill.: InterVarsity Press, 1978.

Photograph Credits

Chapter 1: Beginnings

Chapter 2: The Times They Were A-Changing

Chapter 3: Expansion and Growth

Chapter 4: Years of Transition

Chapter 5: Years of Regrouping

Chapter 6: Moving and Moving Ahead

Chapter 7: The Fryling Years Begin

Chapter 8: Heart. Soul. Mind. Strength.

Name Index

Subject and Title Index